The Careless Society

THE CARELESS SOCIETY

Community and Its Counterfeits

JOHN McKNIGHT

BasicBooks
A Division of HarperCollins*Publishers*

Designed by Joseph Eagle

Library of Congress Cataloging-in-Publication Data
McKnight, John, 1931–
    Careless society : community and its counterfeits / John McKnight.
      p. cm.
    Includes bibliographical references and index.
    ISBN 0–465–09125–3
    1. Community organization—United States. 2. Human services—
United States. 3. United States—Social conditions—1945–
4. Caring. I. Title.
HN58.M35 1995
361.973—dc20   95–1111
                                                  CIP

95 96 97 98 ◆/RRD 9 8 7 6 5 4 3 2

To my parents,
Agness Rose McKnight,
who taught me to love community,
and
John Allen McKnight,
who taught me to seek justice.

Contents

Introduction   *ix*

PROFESSIONALISM
  John Deere and the Bereavement Counselor   3
  The Professional Problem   16
  The Need for Oldness   26
  Professionalized Service and Disabling Help   36

MEDICINE
  The Medicalization of Politics   55
  Well-Being: The New Threshold to the Old Medicine   63
  Diagnosis and the Health of Community   70
  Politicizing Health Care   80

HUMAN SERVICE SYSTEMS
  A Nation of Clients?   91
  Do No Harm   101
  Redefining Community   115
  A Reconsideration of the Crisis of the Welfare State   124

THE CRIMINAL JUSTICE SYSTEM
  Thinking About Crime, Sacrifice, and Community   135
  Rethinking Our National Incarceration Policy   145

On Community
  Community Organizing in the Eighties: Toward a
    Post-Alinsky Agenda *with John Kretzmann*   153
  Regenerating Community   161

Christian Service
  On the Backwardness of Prophets   175

Notes   *181*

Acknowledgments   *185*

Index   *187*

Introduction

How is it that America has become so dispirited? The sense of social disarray is pervasive: families collapsing, schools failing, violence spreading, medical systems out of control, justice systems overwhelmed, prisons burgeoning, human services degenerating, and surveys and studies everywhere indicating the loss of faith of Americans in their basic institutions.

The most common response is a call for institutional reform. Leaders urge Total Quality Management programs, new technologies, "right-sizing," lifelong learning, and new highways for information that will renew the services produced by our systems. The chapters in this book outline the reason that these reforms will fail. And they point toward the path that will allow us to create an effective, satisfying society.

The discussions point out that our problem is not ineffective service-producing institutions. In fact, our institutions are too powerful, authoritative, and strong. Our problem is weak communities, made ever more impotent by our strong service systems.

Those relationships formed by consent and manifested as care are the center of community. It is this consenting care that is the essence of our role as citizens. And it is the ability of citizens to care that creates strong communities and able democracies.

The most significant development transforming America

since World War II has been the growth of a powerful service economy and its pervasive serving institutions. Those institutions have commodified the care of community and called that substitution a service. As citizens have seen the professionalized service commodity invade their communities, they have grown doubtful of their common capacity to care, and so it is that we have become a careless society, populated by impotent citizens and ineffectual communities dependent on the counterfeit of care called human services.

Service systems can never be reformed so they will "produce" care. Care is the consenting commitment of citizens to one another. Care cannot be produced, provided, managed, organized, administered, or commodified. Care is the only thing a system cannot produce. Every institutional effort to replace the real thing is a counterfeit.

Care is, indeed, the manifestation of a community. The community is the site for the relationships of citizens. And it is at this site that the primary work of a caring society must occur. If that site is invaded, co-opted, overwhelmed, and dominated by service-producing institutions, then the work of the community will fail. And that failure is manifest in families collapsing, schools failing, violence spreading, medical systems spinning out of control, justice systems becoming overwhelmed, prisons burgeoning, and human services degenerating.

The chapters in this book were written over the last two decades (1974–1994), when the results of service systems overwhelming communities were coming to dominate our social perceptions. They document the effect of this institutional invasion on various aspects of society, attempting to describe both the futility of the counterfeit and the nature of the authentic care it replaced.

Four counterfeiting aspects of society are analyzed: professionalism, medicine, human service systems, and the criminal justice system.

The section on professionalism involves an examination of those societal agents who announce to citizens and their communities, "You will be better because we know better." In a single statement they destroy the sense of community competence by capturing and commodifying the citizens' capacity to solve problems and to care.

The section on medicine examines the vanguard force of the institutional invasion of community life. The physicians and the medical systems that have grown up around them are the models and exemplars for all the other professionals seeking imperial prerogatives. And this in spite of the overwhelming proof of the medical system's peripheral influence on how long we live and how often we are sick. Therefore, this section concludes with a report on the discovery by citizens in one neighborhood that their health is a reflection of their community capacity and not the dazzling but medically careless counterfeit.

The section on human service systems describes their developing skills in client-making. "Do No Harm" provides a theoretical framework for defining the inherent structurally harmful consequences of all service system interventions. The section concludes with "A Reconsideration of the Crisis of the Welfare State" describing how the progress of the client-making process finally creates a community culture of its own. This culture, which replaces community with management, stories with curriculum, and care with commodities, is the serviced society—a careless place dominated by impotent institutions and burgeoning social pathology.

The section on the criminal justice system is intended to remind us that the prodigious growth of this service system is the consequence of communities grown impotent in the face of the cultural dominance and economic monopoly of the other service systems.

Following the sections on the systems that counterfeit the manifestations of community, a section on community points toward the nature and growth of authentic citizen communities of care.

In the West, the ideological roots of service grow from the institutionalization of a religious ideal. Therefore, the book concludes with a reflection on the ideal of Christian service and its transformation into carelessness.

The ideas in this book grew out of forty years of work in the urban neighborhoods of North America. There I observed the gradual transformation of many lower-income neighborhoods from citizen-powered communities to institutions without walls. Where the transformation did not occur, it was consistently the result of the vigorous defense and assertion of the capacity, concern, commitment, and care of communities of citizens.

Initially, I did not understand that competent communities could be invaded, captured, and colonized by professionalized services. However, through these decades seven people helped me understand the struggle I was observing.

The first was Saul Alinsky, whose *Reveille for Radicals* I read at the age of fifteen when it was first published. His political vision of communities controlled by citizens and their associations first gave names and a map to the reality of my everyday life.

Ivan Illich, a man of great brilliance, perspective, and heart, adopted me. On our journey, I was an intellectual waif, but he patiently told me the stories of our past that explained the present and predicted the future. Standing outside our culture, he helped me see the nature, wealth, and culturally mediated tragedy of a society where technology is not God and communities are home.

Robert Mendelsohn, a physician and friend, came to see his own medical work and world as a false religion. He shared his insights with me. They became a revelation and then his book, *Confessions of a Medical Heretic.* His diagnosis of our ills was "lack of community," and his prescription was "What would your grandmother say?"

Robert Rodale, president of Rodale Press, was a gentle, humble, precious colleague. He was rooted in the earth and explored with me nature's regenerative code. Together, through that metaphor, we rediscovered the nature of the healing powers of communities. He led me to travel beyond critique, seeking rediscovery of the seeds of community regeneration.

Jerome Miller, now president of the National Center for Institutions and Alternatives, became a friend while he was exploring the unknown beyond institutions. He is clearly America's most significant modern social explorer. In his 1991 book, *Last One Over the Wall*, he documents a remarkable expedition in which he became responsible for hundreds of young people in juvenile correction institutions. The results of his liberation of these people from their jailer-servers is a unique report of the world on the other side of the professional paradigm.

Robert Woodson, president of the National Center for Neighborhood Enterprise, has seen the professional invasion of neighborhoods across America. His initiatives to create a citizen counterforce have been a powerful antidote to the disabling effects of colonizing human service systems. I have learned a great deal from his hopeful struggle in the streets of America's cities.

Since my first year of college, Franklyn Haiman, Professor Emeritus of Communication Studies at Northwestern University, has been my mentor. His faith in democracy and civil liberty shaped forever my understanding of the nature of a citizen.

Many colleagues at Northwestern University's Center for Urban Affairs and Policy Research joined and enlightened me over the years these ideas were developed. I am especially indebted to Paul Arntson, Malcolm Bush, Rosita De La Rosa, Tom Dewar, Andrew Gordon, Stan Hallett, John Kretzmann, Arthur Lyons, and Steven Whitman.

Finally, as these essays were written, my closest daily working associate has been Alice Murray. She has directed my office all these years and reminded me by her wondrous way that care is gracious, calm, and filled with dignity.

Evanston, Illinois
September 1994

Professionalism

John Deere and the Bereavement Counselor

In 1973, E. F. Schumacher startled Western societies with a revolutionary economic analysis that found that small is beautiful. His book of the same name concluded with these words: "The guidance we need . . . cannot be found in science or technology, the value of which utterly depends on the ends they serve; but it can still be found in the traditional wisdom of mankind."

Because traditional wisdom is passed on through stories rather than studies, it seems appropriate that this chapter should start with a story.

The story begins as the European pioneers crossed the Alleghenies and started to settle the Midwest. The land they found was covered with forests. With great effort they felled the trees, pulled up the stumps, and planted their crops in the rich, loamy soil.

When they finally reached the western edge of the place we now call Indiana, the forest stopped and ahead lay a thousand miles of the great grass prairie. The Europeans were puzzled by this new environment. Some even called it the Great Desert. It seemed untillable. The earth was often very wet and it was covered with centuries of tangled and matted grasses.

The settlers found that the prairie sod could not be cut with their cast-iron plows, and that the wet earth stuck to their plowshares. Even a team of the best oxen bogged down after a few yards of tugging. The iron plow was a useless tool to farm the prairie soil. The pioneers were stymied for nearly two decades. Their western march was halted and they filled in the eastern regions of the Midwest.

In 1837, a blacksmith in the town of Grand Detour, Illinois, invented a new tool. His name was John Deere, and the tool was a plow made of steel. It was sharp enough to cut through matted grasses and smooth enough to cast off the mud. It was a simple tool, the "sodbuster," that opened the great prairies to agricultural development.

Sauk County, Wisconsin, is the part of that prairie where I have a home. It is named after the Sauk Indians. In 1673, Father Marquette was the first European to lay his eyes upon their land. He found a village laid out in regular patterns on a plain beside the Wisconsin River. He called the place Prairie du Sac. The village was surrounded by fields that had provided maize, beans, and squash for the Sauk people for generations reaching back into unrecorded time.

When the European settlers arrived at the Sauk Prairie in 1837, the government forced the native Sauk people west of the Mississippi River. The settlers came with John Deere's new invention and used the tool to open the area to a new kind of agriculture. They ignored the traditional ways of the Sauk Indians and used their sodbusting tool for planting wheat.

Initially, the soil was generous and the farmers thrived. However, each year the soil lost more of its nurturing power. It was only thirty years after the Europeans arrived with their new technology that the land was depleted. Wheat farming became uneconomical and tens of thousands of farmers left Wisconsin seeking new land with sod to bust.

It took the Europeans and their new technology just one generation to make their homeland into a desert. The Sauk Indians, who knew how to sustain themselves on the Sauk Prairie, were banished to another kind of desert called a reservation. And even they forgot about the techniques and tools that had sustained them on the prairie for generations.

And that is how it was that three deserts were created: Wisconsin, the reservation, and the memories of a people.

A century and a half later, the land of the Sauks is now populated by the children of a second wave of European farmers who learned to replenish the soil through the regenerative powers of dairying, ground-cover crops, and animal manures. These third- and fourth-generation farmers and townspeople do not realize, however, that a new settler is coming soon with an invention as powerful as John Deere's plow.

The new technology is called "bereavement counseling." It is a tool forged at the great state university, an innovative technique to meet the needs of those experiencing the death of a loved one, a tool that can "process" the grief of the people who now live on the Prairie of the Sauk.

As one can imagine the final days of the village of the Sauk Indians before the arrival of the settlers with John Deere's plow, one can also imagine these final days before the arrival of the first bereavement counselor at Prairie du Sac. In these final days, the farmers and the townspeople mourn the death of a mother, brother, son, or friend. The bereaved are joined by neighbors and kin. They meet grief together in lamentation, prayer, and song. They call upon the words of the clergy and surround themselves with community.

It is in these ways that they grieve and then go on with life. Through their mourning they are assured of the bonds between them and renewed in the knowledge that this death is a part of the past and the future of the people on the Prairie of the Sauk. Their grief is common property, an anguish from which the community draws strength and which gives it the courage to move ahead.

Into this prairie community the bereavement counselor arrives with the new grief technology. The counselor calls the invention a service and assures the prairie folk of its effectiveness and superiority by invoking the name of the great university while displaying a diploma and license.

At first, we can imagine that the local people will be puzzled by the bereavement counselor's claims. However, the counselor will tell a few of them that the new technique is merely to *assist* the bereaved's community at the time of death. To some other prairie folk who are isolated or forgotten, the counselor will offer help in grief processing. These lonely souls will accept the intervention, mistaking the counselor for a friend.

For those who are penniless, the counselor will approach the County Board and advocate the "right to treatment" for these unfortunate souls. This right will be guaranteed by the Board's decision to reimburse those too poor to pay for counseling services.

There will be others, schooled to believe in the innovative new tools certified by universities and medical centers, who will seek out the bereavement counselor by force of habit. And one of these people will tell a bereaved neighbor who is unschooled that unless his grief is processed by a counselor, he will probably have major psychological problems in later life.

Several people will begin to contact the bereavement counselor because, since the County Board now taxes them to *ensure* access to the technology, they will feel that to fail to be counseled is to waste their money and to be denied a benefit, or even a right.

Finally, one day the aged father of a local woman will die. And the next-door neighbor will not drop by because he doesn't want to interrupt the bereavement counselor. The woman's kin will stay home because they will have learned that only the bereavement counselor knows how to process grief in the proper way. The local clergy will seek technical assistance from the bereavement counselor to learn the correct form of service to deal with guilt and grief. And the grieving daughter will know that it is the bereavement counselor who *really* cares for her, because only the bereavement counselor appears when death visits this family on the Prairie of the Sauk.

It will be only one generation between the time the bereavement counselor arrives and the disappearance of the community of mourners. The counselor's new tool will cut through the social fabric, throwing aside kinship, care, neighborly obligations, and community ways of coming together and going on. Like John Deere's plow, the tools of bereavement counseling will create a desert where a community once flourished.

And finally, even the bereavement counselor will see the impossibility of restoring hope in clients once they are genuinely alone, with nothing but a service for consolation. In the inevitable failure of the service, the bereavement counselor will find the desert even in herself.

There are those who would say that neither John Deere nor the bereavement counselor has created a desert. Rather, they would argue that these new tools have great benefits and that we have focused unduly upon a few negative side effects. Indeed, they might agree with Eli Lilly, founder of the famous drug company, whose motto was "A drug without side effects is no drug at all."

To those with this perspective, the critical issue is the amelioration or correction of the negative effects. In Lilly's idiom, they can conceive of a new drowsiness-creating pill designed to overcome the nausea created by an anticancer drug. They envision a prairie scattered with pyramids of new technologies and techniques, each designed to correct the error of its predecessor, but none without its own error to be corrected. In building these pyramids, they will also recognize the unlimited opportunities for research, development, and badly needed employment. Indeed, many will name this pyramiding process "progress" and note its positive effect upon the gross national product.

The countervailing view holds that these pyramiding service technologies are now counterproductive constructions, essentially impediments rather than monuments.

E. F. Schumacher helped clarify for many of us the nature of those physical tools that are so counterproductive that they become impediments. There is an increasing recognition of the waste and devastation created by these new physical tools, from nuclear generators to supersonic transports. They are the sons and daughters of the sodbuster.

It is much less obvious that the bereavement counselor is

also the sodbuster's heir. It is more difficult for us to see how service technology creates deserts. Indeed, there are even those who argue that a good society should scrap its nuclear generators in order to recast them into plowshares of service. They would replace the counterproductive *goods* technology with the *service* technology of modern medical centers, universities, correctional systems, and nursing homes. It is essential, therefore, that we have new measures of service technologies that will allow us to distinguish those that are impediments from those that are monuments.

We can assess the degree of impediment incorporated in modern service technologies by weighing four basic elements. The first is the monetary cost. At what point do the economics of a service technology consume enough of the commonwealth that all of society becomes eccentric and distorted?

Schumacher helped us recognize the radical social, political, and environmental distortions created by huge investments in covering our land with concrete in the name of transportation. Similarly, we are now investing 12 percent of our national wealth in "health care technology" that blankets most of our communities with a medicalized understanding of well-being. As a result, we now imagine that there are mutant human beings called health consumers. We create costly "health-making" environments that are usually large, windowless rooms filled with immobile adult bicycles and dreadfully heavy objects purported to benefit one if they are lifted.

The second element to be weighed was identified by Ivan Illich as "specific counterproductivity." Beyond the negative side effect is the possibility that a service technology can produce the specific inverse of its stated purpose. Thus, one can imagine sickening medicine, stupidifying schools, and crime-making corrections systems.

The evidence grows that some service technologies are now so counterproductive that their abolition is the most productive means to achieve the goal for which they were initially established. Take, for example, the experiment in Massachusetts where, under the leadership of Dr. Jerome Miller, the juvenile correction institutions were closed. As the most recent evalua-tion studies indicate, the Massachusetts recidivism rate has declined while comparable states with increasing institutional-ized populations see an increase in youthful criminality.

There is also the discomforting fact that during doctor strikes in Israel, Canada, and the United States, the death rate took an unprecedented plunge.

Perhaps the most telling example of specifically counterpro-ductive service technologies is demonstrated by the Medicaid program, which provides "health care for the poor." In most states, the amount expended for medical care for the poor is now greater than the cash welfare income provided for that same poor population. Thus, a low-income mother is given $1.00 in income and $1.50 in medical care. It is perfectly clear that the single greatest cause of her ill health is her low in-come. Nonetheless, the response to her sickening poverty is an ever-growing investment in medical technology—an invest-ment that now consumes her income.

The third element to be weighed is the loss of knowledge. Many of the settlers who came to Wisconsin with John Deere's sodbuster had been peasant farmers in Europe. There, they had tilled the land for centuries using methods that replen-ished its nourishing capacity. However, once the land seemed unlimited and John Deere's technology came to dominate, they forgot the tools and methods that had sustained them for centuries in the old land and created a new desert.

The same process is at work with the modern service tech-nologies and the professions that use them. One of the most vivid examples involves the methods of a new breed of technol-ogists called pediatricians and obstetricians. During the first half of the twentieth century, these technocrats came, quite naturally, to believe that the preferred method of feeding ba-bies was with a manufactured formula rather than breast milk. Acting as agents for the new lactation technology, these pro-fessionals persuaded a generation of women to abjure breast-feeding in favor of their more "healthful" way.

In the fifties in a Chicago suburb, there was a woman named

Marion Thompson who still remembered that babies could be fed by breast as well as by can. However, she could find no professional to advise her. She searched for someone who might still remember something about the process of breastfeeding. Fortunately, she found one woman whose memory included the information necessary to begin the flow of milk. From that faint memory, breastfeeding began its long struggle toward restoration in our society. She and six friends started a club that multiplied itself into thousands of small communities and became an international association of women dedicated to breastfeeding: La Leche League. This popular movement reversed the technological imperative in only one generation and has established breastfeeding as a norm in spite of the countervailing views of the service technologists.

Indeed, the American Academy of Pediatrics finally took the official position that breastfeeding is preferable to nurturing infants from canned products. It was as though the Sauk Indians had recovered the Wisconsin prairie and allowed it once again to nourish a people with popular tools.

The fourth element to be weighed is the "hidden curriculum" of the service technologies. As they are implemented through professional techniques, the invisible message of the interaction between professional and client is, "You will be better because I know better." As these professional techniques proliferate across the social landscape, they represent a new praxis, an ever-growing pedagogy that teaches this basic message of the service technologies. Through the propagation of belief in authoritative expertise, professionals cut through the social fabric of community and sow clienthood where citizenship once grew.

It is clear, therefore, that to assess the purported benefits of service technologies, they must be weighed against the sum of the socially distorting monetary costs to the commonwealth; the inverse effects of the interventions; the loss of knowledge, tools, and skills regarding other ways; and the antidemocratic consciousness created by a nation of clients. When the benefits are weighed in this balance, we can begin to recognize how often the tools of professionalized service make social deserts where communities once bloomed.

Unfortunately, the bereavement counselor is but one of many new professionalized servicers that plow over our communities like John Deere's sodbusting settlers. These new technologists have now occupied much of the community's space and represent a powerful force for colonizing the remaining social relations. Nonetheless, resistance against this invasion can still be seen in local community struggles against the designs of planners, parents' unions demanding control over their children's learning, women's groups struggling to reclaim their medicalized bodies, and community efforts to settle disputes and conflicts by stealing the property claimed by lawyers.

Frequently, as in the case of La Leche League, this decolonization effort is successful. Often, however, the resistance fails and the new service technologies transform citizens and their communities into social deserts grown over with a scrub brush of clients and consumers.

This process is reminiscent of the final English conquest of Scotland after the Battle of Culloden. The English were convinced by a history of repeated uprisings that the Scottish tribes would never be subdued. Therefore, after the battle, the English killed many of the clansmen and forced the rest from their small crofts into the coastal towns, where there was little work and no choice but to emigrate. Great Britain was freed of the tribal threat. The clans were decimated and their lands given to the English lords, who grazed sheep where communities once flourished. My Scots ancestors said of this final solution of the Anglo-Saxon, "They created a desert and called it freedom."

One can hear echoes of this understanding in today's social deserts, where modern "Anglo-Saxons" declare the advantages of exiled clienthood, describing it as self-fulfillment, individual development, self-realization, and other mirages of autonomy.

Our modern experience with service technologies tells us that it is difficult to recapture professionally occupied space. We have also learned that whenever that space is liberated, it is even more difficult to construct a new social order that will not be quickly co-opted again.

A vivid current example is the unfortunate trend developing within the hospice movement. In the United States, those who created the movement were attempting to detechnologize dying—to wrest death from the hospital and allow it to occur within the family.

Since the movement began in the 1970s, we have seen the rapid growth of "hospital-based hospices" and new legislation reimbursing those hospices that will formally tie themselves to hospitals and employ physicians as central "caregivers."

The professional co-optation of community efforts to invent appropriate techniques for citizens to care in the community has been pervasive. We need to identify the characteristics of those social forms that are resistant to colonization by service technologies while enabling communities to cultivate care. These authentic social forms are characterized by three basic dimensions: They tend to be *uncommodified, unmanaged,* and *uncurricularized.*

The tools of the bereavement counselor have made grief into a *commodity* rather than an opportunity for community. Service technologies convert conditions into commodities, and care into service.

The tools of the *manager* convert communality into hierarchy, replacing consent with control. Where once there was a commons, the manager creates a corporation.

The tools of the *pedagogue* create monopolies in place of cultures. By making a school of everyday life, community definitions and citizen action are degraded and finally expelled.

It is this hardworking team—the service professional, the manager, and the pedagogue—that pulls the tools of "community-busting" through the modern social landscape. Therefore, if we are to recultivate community, we will need to return this team to the stable, abjuring their use.

How will we learn again to cultivate community? Schumacher concluded that "the guidance we need . . . can still be found in the traditional wisdom." Therefore, we can return to those who understand how to allow the Sauk Prairie to bloom and sustain a people.

One of their leaders, a chief of the Sauk, was named Blackhawk. After his people were exiled to the land west of the Mississippi and their resistance movement was broken at the Battle of Bad Axe, Blackhawk said of the prairie:

> There, we always had plenty; our children never cried from hunger, neither were our people in want. The rapids of our river furnished us with an abundance of excellent fish and the land, being very fertile, never failed to produce good crops of corn, beans, pumpkins, and squash. Here our village stood for more than a hundred years. Our village was healthy and there was no place in the country possessing such advantages, nor hunting grounds better than ours. If a prophet had come to our village in those days and told us that the things were to take place which have since come to pass, none of our people would have believed the prophecy.

But the settlers came with their new tools and the prophecy was fulfilled. One of Blackhawk's Wintu sisters described the result:

> The white people never cared for land or deer or bear. When we kill meat, we eat it all. When we dig roots, we make little holes. When we build houses, we make little holes. When we burn grass for grasshoppers, we don't ruin things. We shake down acorns and pinenuts. We don't chop down trees. We only use dead weed. But the whites plow up the ground, pull down the trees, kill everything.
>
> The tree says, "Don't. I am sore. Don't hurt me!" But they chop it down and cut it up.

The spirit of the land hates them. They blast out trees
and stir it up to its depths. They saw up the trees. That
hurts them. . . . They blast rocks and scatter them on the
ground. The rock says, "Don't. You are hurting me!" But
the white people pay no attention. When [we] use rocks,
we take only little round ones for cooking. . . .

How can the spirit of the earth like the white man?
Everywhere they have touched the earth, it is sore.

Blackhawk and his Wintu sister tell us that the land has a
Spirit. Their community on the prairie, their ecology, was a
people guided by that Spirit.

When John Deere's people came to the Sauk Prairie, they
exorcised the Prairie Spirit in the name of a new god, Technology. Because it was a god of their making, they believed they
were gods.

And they made a desert.

There are incredible possibilities if we are willing to fail to
be gods.

This chapter, imagining the advent of bereavement counselors
in the Sauk Prairie, was written in October 1984. On September 18, 1986, the following article appeared in the *Sauk-
Prairie Star*, the newspaper for the citizens of Sauk Prairie.

GRIEVING WILL BE SEMINAR TOPIC

Sauk Prairie High School guidance staff will present a
seminar on grieving for freshmen and seniors at Sauk
Prairie High School during the week of September
22–26. The seminar is being presented due to the recent
losses of classmates for students in the classes of 1990 and
1987.

Freshmen will attend the seminar in conjunction with
required health classes. Students who have no health

classes first semester will be assigned a presentation during study halls.

Seniors will attend the seminar in conjunction with family living classes. Students who do not have a family living class will be assigned a presentation.

Parents are welcome to call the Guidance Center to discuss any concerns they may have. Parents must authorize students not attending the seminars.

The Professional Problem

Revolutions begin when people who are defined as problems achieve the power to redefine the problem.

A critical point in the development of the civil rights struggle was the black movement's capacity to declare the central issue the "White problem." A people declared deficient and in need unshackled their labels and attempted to lock them on their oppressors.

There was a revolutionary insight in that strategy. It recognized that the power to label people deficient and declare them in need is the basic tool of control and oppression in modern industrialized societies of democratic and totalitarian persuasions. The agents with comprehensive labeling power in these societies are the helping professionals. Their badge bestows the caring authority to declare their fellow citizens "clients"— a class of deficient people in need.

As was the case with the black revolution, we can now see signs of "client populations" beginning to wonder whether they are really the problem. One manifestation of this client uneasiness is the self-help movement. This movement is peopled by many ex-clients who have understood the limits of their professional helpers and/or the disabling effects of their services. The angriest and most political are repeating the black redefinition of the sixties. They reject their clienthood and seek liberation by defining the problem as those who have defined them as the problem. To these ex-clients, the central issue is the "professional problem."

Their once-lonely struggle to proclaim the "professional problem" has been aided by a growing chorus of voices. Radical social critics such as Ivan Illich have defined the iatrogenic capacities of professionals.[1] Peter Berger and Richard Neuhaus have described the decay of primary social structures facilitated by modern professionalism.[2] Eli Ginzberg worries that the new class of professionals may usurp the decision-making power within our industrial structure.[3] Jacques Barzun concludes that if our professions are to survive with their traditional freedom, a major recovery of mental and moral force will be necessary.[4] Even Nathan Glazer is attracted by the attack on the professionals and hesitantly commends its best spokesmen for their insight.[5] And President Jimmy Carter specifically attacked the lawyers and the doctors of America, sensing that the "professional problem" was a popular political issue.

The growing critique suggests that critical issues of power and control must be at stake. Paradoxically, the two most obvious interests involved in the attack on professionals are those who oppose the growth of government and those who would increase the role of government.

The antigovernment interests depend upon an automatic popular translation of "professional" into "government bureaucrat." While significant numbers of professionals are state employees or funded by the state, there are obvious distinctions between a professional and a bureaucratic class. Nonetheless, the conservative uses of the "professional problem" are clearly focused on attacking big, bureaucratic government. The fact that this translation is so dependable suggests that both classes may have a common characteristic in the popular mind—the production of paid non-work.

The progovernment interests use the "professional problem" to defend the state and its bureaucracy by making the distinction between the professional and bureaucratic classes.

They typically suggest that inflated public budgets are really caused by "greedy doctors" at the Medicare-Medicaid trough or "self-serving teachers" consuming ever more of the public wealth while school populations and standard achievement scores decrease.

Major corporations have also joined in professional-baiting. The Benefits Director of General Motors complains that the company's cost of medical insurance is greater than the price of all the steel it uses to build automobiles. Corporate managers universally complain of their increasing dependence on growing cadres of lawyers. Indeed, their public rhetoric suggests that corporate leaders no longer view unions as their principal burden. Instead, they are beginning to define the "professional problem/bureaucracy" as the monkey on their back.

Some representatives of the poor and minorities have also joined the attack on professionals. Welfare recipient organizations complain that their professional servicers now receive more money for their help than the recipients receive in cash grants. In many states, for example, the Medicaid budget for medical service to welfare recipients is now larger than the budget for direct cash grants to those recipients. Like the corporations, many advocates of the underclass describe themselves as victims of the "professional problem"—poor people defined as deficient by those whose incomes depend upon the deficiency they define.

When presidents, intellectuals, conservatives, liberals, corporations, and the poor join in common cause against a class of workers numbering fourteen million Americans, it is time that we examine the causes of the "professional problem." The current analysts suggest three basic causes for the revolt against the professional "problem definers."

The first cause is the inefficiency argument. This position suggests that the professionals are being attacked because they are doing less with more. Teachers receive much more of the GNP while student achievement scores decline. The medical professions consume one-ninth of the GNP while their interventions have little effect upon life expectancy. The number of lawyers doubles as the popular sense of injustice multiplies. Criminal justice systems expand as the perception of personal security declines.

There is hardly a professionalized service that has not received an increasing portion of the GNP during the last decade. Nonetheless, the problems they have defined as their jurisdiction have consistently grown worse in public perceptions. In managerial terms, inputs are up and outputs are down. In investor idiom, there is no leverage. In taxpayer language, it's a bad "proposition."

Inefficiency is an attractive argument because it is based upon American pragmatism. It explains the revolt against the professional as the simple rejection of something that isn't working. Its proponents are not much concerned with the reasons for the nonproductivity, but they are clear that they will not pay more for less. Therefore, the budget analyst, the manager, and the cost-cutters are being engaged to trim the professional fat.

The second cause of the revolt is explained by the arrogance argument. This position suggests that the nature of profession is inherently elitist and dominant. Given the professional powers to define problems, treat them, and evaluate the efficacy of the treatment, the client as a person has been a residual category in the process. As professions have become integrated into large-scale specialized systems, financed by public funds and insurance plans, the professional has increasingly secured a guaranteed annual income. The consequence is that the client's residual role as a volitional purchaser of service, or even as a human being in need, has disappeared and the professional is free to use the client without pretense of humanistic service. The resulting arrogance, magnified by the modernized systems of assembly-line, multiservice "care" that institutionalize the individual professional, has evoked the consumer movements.

These consumer reform efforts are, at the least, client efforts to develop enough counterpower to require professionals to treat clients like human beings, if not equals. Patient advocates, parent groups, and client councils are political efforts to remedy professional arrogance.

The arrogance argument is attractive because it suggests that the "professional problem" can be resolved if we reinstate the humanistic traditions of professional work. The consumer vehicle for this rehumanization is, paradoxically, advocacy, adversarial and confrontational in its nature. It suggests that we can somehow *force* professionals to *care* again. Consumer-oriented reformers are therefore instituting new professional training curricula that attempt to *teach* professionals to care. The result is exemplified by a consumer group that manages to coerce a medical school to *require* all students to take courses in humanistic/wholistic health care.

The third explanation for the "professional problem" is the iatrogenic argument. While the inefficiency argument suggests that the problem is that professionals don't work, the ia-trogenicists argue that they do work—but to our detriment. This position holds that the negative side effects of technological, specialized professionalism are so harmful to so many that the revolt is the reaction to professionally administered injury.

The injury comes in several forms that are brilliantly defined by Ivan Illich in his book *Medical Nemesis*.[6] Afflicted with sick-producing medicine, stupidifying education, and criminalizing justice, the citizen reacts with an inchoate anger. Incredulous that schools could "produce" ignorance and hospitals "manufacture" malady, the citizen/client strikes out in blind outrage. The professionals and their technological and intellectual allies counterattack by calling the popular outrage "know-nothingism," "anti-intellectualism," and "a turn to the right."

Nonetheless, such diverse intellects as Peter Berger and Richard Neuhaus have supported the iatrogenic argument with their description of negative effects of professional dominance upon the problem-solving capacities of the primary social structures of society: family, neighborhood, church/synagogue, ethnic group, voluntary associations, and popular political parties.[7] And historian Christopher Lasch adds his voice by describing the family as a victim of the professional serving as a capitalist vanguard commodifying the nonworking time of Americans to ensure new markets.[8]

The iatrogenic argument is the least attractive of the three causal propositions because it suggests that helpers hurt. The very idea offends the mind. Nonetheless, the disabling experience with professionals creates frustrations that must be expressed. For those who cannot speak the unspeakable, who cannot define the problem as those who have defined them as the problem, the alternatives include collapse into personal guilt, escape into narcissistic cults, or the numbing possibilities of licit and illicit drugs. The ultimate tragedy of each of these responses to professional iatrogenesis is that professionals feed on them. They stand ready to help again with the guilt, narcissism, or drug use. Like a hall of mirrors, the problem definer creates the treatment that creates the problem and creates the remedy. . . .

What do we do about this increasingly inefficient, arrogant, and iatrogenic class? Jacques Barzun notes the urgency of the issue by concluding that "without . . . heroic effort, we professionals shall all go down—appropriately—as non-heroes together."[9]

All three explanations for the "professional problem" imply the possibility of reform by re-creating an economic, democratic, and efficacious practice. Here and there, one sees serious, if fragile, efforts to reform professional practice. Its labels are eclectic: humanistic medicine, free schools, community dispute settlement, (w)holistic health care, community-based care. Whatever the label, the common perception of the reformers is that a heroic effort can rectify professionalism and create a new class of professionals in the useful service of humanity.

It is my view that this vision is neither possible nor desirable. The hopeful future for helping work is more likely to result from the fall of the modernized professions and the development of new definitions of good work.

Professional reform is unlikely because our current approaches to economic growth and national stability *depend* upon the development of more professionalized service of the same kind we are currently experiencing. In 1900, approximately 10 percent of the paid workforce "produced" services. Daniel Bell's projections suggest that by the year 2000, the service workforce will represent 90 percent of the employed. If his projections are correct, during the twentieth century, nearly 80 percent of America's work will have been translated from goods to service "production" jobs. This translation will provide jobs for two of the major groups that are entering the workforce during the latter half of the century—women leaving the homeforce and the graduates of higher education with expensive postgraduate degrees that promise them professional roles.

All of the forces in our economy are now programmed to create a geometric increase in the number of professionals while the goods production sector is designed to replace the labor of Americans with machines and foreign labor. The government must increase the GNP and "control" unemployment. There seems to be no choice but to pump up the service economy. The choice is easy because the more privileged of our society—college graduates and homeworkers entering the paid labor force—expect the prestige accorded professional work. Therefore, the development of a professionalized workforce is the economic keystone of our highly educated, technologized society as long as we are committed to two propositions:

1. A growing GNP is good.
2. The "production" of professional service adds to the GNP.

In our drive to increase professionalized service "production," there is a popular assumption that we are intensifying the good works of society. With more professionals we will kill cancer, make the criminal justice system work, learn how to teach reading, cure deafness, and give sight to the blind.

There is, on the other hand, a contradictory popular insight that doubts that we really need more professionals. There are not many Americans who believe that doubling the number of lawyers will decrease either injustice or crime. There are serious doubts that we need more teachers or social workers in a population with decreasing numbers of young people. And the high priests of medicine are confronted by popular doubt through the malpractice rebellion.

Obviously, Americans are ambivalent and confused about the impacts of professional proliferation. In spite of this confusion, it is clear that the direction of professional growth is at the *margin* of perceived problems. A careful analysis of the recent areas of professional development indicates that "unmet needs" are the growth sector of the service industry. The most recent discovery of these new "needs" include "tired housewife syndrome," "six-hour retardation" (a child who is normal for the 18 hours a day not in school), "bereavement deficit" (previously known as grief), "incipient child abuse" (the possibility that a parent might hurt a child), "litigative incapacity" (the lack of funds to sue others to secure equity), and "reclusiveness" (the desire not to associate with others).

Each of these new discoveries of unmet "needs" creates a "demand" for a new profession. At least one major university is now training graduates to meet the needs of people with "bereavement deficits" by providing a master's degree in Bereavement Counseling (MBC). The practitioners of this developing profession have organized a professional association whose first goal is to lobby for clauses in public and private life insurance policies that would guarantee their services for the kin of the deceased.

Those who are infected by "reclusiveness" have called forth a new profession in at least one major city. These professionals are tentatively called "recluse managers." Their services include identifying recluses, maintaining inconspicuous surveillance, and, at the proper moment prescribed by strict professional standards, intervening in the life of the recluse.

It is now clear that the economic pressure to professionalize requires an expanding universe of need and the magnification of deficiency. This form of marginal professional development can only intensify the ineffective, dominating, and iatrogenic nature of the professional class as they invade the remaining perimeters of personhood.

To suggest that we can reform bereavement counselors and recluse managers is a profound misunderstanding of the current "professional problem." The basic issue is profession itself, dependent upon the manufacture of need and the definition of new deficiencies. One can imagine that the modern "professional problem" will be resolved when the lives of enough people are so completely invaded by the professional need for deficiency that a popular revolt develops.

There is, however, another possibility for change that I can verify only by my personal experience. Since 1975 I have spoken to numerous professional associations regarding the degrading professional "manufacture of need" and the iatrogenic effects of professionalized service. While one might expect a negative reaction to this message, the response by professionals in subsequent question periods, workshops, and dialogue sessions is almost always positive. Instead of an argument, I find professionals consistently giving me examples of their own useless and iatrogenic activities.

To my great surprise, I am not asked, "How can I do a better job?" Instead, the constant question, asked especially by younger people, is, "What do you think I could do that would be worth doing?"*

It is this subversive question in the minds of so many young professionals that suggests the possibility for radical change. They are not arguing that their professional work can or should be reformed. Their poignant inquiry recognizes that

---

*There is one qualification. Lawyers, social workers, psychologists, planners, social service workers, teachers, and youth workers ask this question. Most doctors do not. They are the remaining "true believers," the professional zealots of our time.

they know how useless, controlling, exploitative, or harmful is the central function of their work.

They are too honest to ask about reform. Their question is, "Can you tell me what good work needs to be done in America? I thought that professional training would lead me to good work, but it has led me to live off some people who don't need me and others I can't help."

The politics for a new definition of legitimate work in America may grow from the confluence of citizens angered by the professional invasion of personhood and young professionals disillusioned by lives wasted in the manufacture of need. The possibility for this politics requires an economy that can provide legitimate work for all those people who do not want to make a living by creating deficiencies in their neighbors.

What is legitimate work? What is worth doing? What is good work for America's people?

The answer to these questions takes us beyond the idea of profession. Our possibilities are hopeful if we can envision a society with good work to be done that does not waste our people in the proliferation of profession.

Can you tell me what good work needs to be done in America? The answer will dissolve the "professional problem."

The Need for Oldness

The United States is finally becoming a caring country. Shocked by assassinations, Vietnam, Watergate, and "stagflation," our people have turned to caring as the one ideal that cannot be corrupted.

Young people flock to schools of medicine, law, social work, and urban planning. Two-thirds of our people derive their income from delivering services that are mainly caring.

The American caring that is growing most rapidly is service to the old. Our aging population is increasing so rapidly that a caring society can no longer ignore the "seniors." Lawyers, doctors, social workers, psychiatrists, physical therapists, counselors, and housing officials are now directing their care and concern to the old.

Concern for the elderly has resulted in an increasing professionalization of those who care for the old. This professional concern was expressed by the title of a national conference convened by a major midwestern university: "Frontiers in Aging: Life Extension." The seven hundred participants were caring professionals from all the disciplines that help the aging.

Having been asked to speak to this group, I immediately consulted my mother-in-law. She is eighty-one years of age, comes from a Lithuanian background, and lives in an apartment near our home.

We call my mother-in-law Old Grandma. She likes that name because she believes it makes her an authority.

When I told her that a conference called "Frontiers in Aging: Life Extension" was about her, she shook her head. She couldn't imagine they were talking about her because their language is of a different order than the words that Old Grandma knows.

Words like "frontiers," "aging," and "extension" are about *going, becoming,* and *moving forward.* Old Grandma doesn't think those words relate to her life. To her, old is *being.* When Old Grandma says "old," it isn't good or bad. "Old" is like saying she's a woman. It is a condition, a state. To her, old is something that is not associated with problems. A problem is how to get the janitor to get the steam heat up to the right temperature. But old isn't a problem.

For Old Grandma, old is:

    . . . finally knowing what is important.
    . . . when you are, rather than when you are becoming.
    . . . knowing about pain rather than fearing it.
    . . . being able to gain more pleasure from memory than
        from prospect.
    . . . when doctors become impotent and powerless.
    . . . when satisfaction depends less and less on consumption.
    . . . using the strength that a good life has stored for you.
    . . . enjoying deference.
    . . . worrying about irrelevance.

Old Grandma's "old" cannot be counted. Therefore, people who count things will never know about her old. They are trapped by the tools of counting. The economists, social scientists, census-takers, and actuaries are closed out of her world because they can't count what counts to her.

Old Grandma wonders about the problem of people who have a conference on "old." She thinks that there is a problem with people who think old is a problem.

Old Grandma is supported in her view by a famous physician named Lewis Thomas, former dean of the Yale Medical School and president of the Memorial Sloan-Kettering Cancer Center. In a 1975 article he noted that our life expectancy had reached seventy-two years and less than 1 percent of us died each year. He went on to suggest that the major problem in the United States, in terms of health, was that we are becoming a nation of hypochondriacs.

Here we are, a people now living past seventy-two years, and we hold conferences called "Frontiers of Aging: Life Extension." Old Grandma cannot understand that. To her, the conference is a problem.

Unfortunately, Old Grandma is wrong in thinking old is not a problem. Old Grandma doesn't understand that old is a problem because she has never understood the gross national product! The gross national product is a number that we have been led to believe is the best indicator of how well we are doing as a society. It is a number made up of two parts. One part is the number counting the production of goods. The other part is the number counting the production of services. Each year we want that two-part number to be bigger if we are to be a better society.

In 1900, when Old Grandma was three years old, her job was to wipe the blood from her father's boots when he came home from the slaughterhouse. That year, 90 percent of the people in the United States who were working for an income were making things and 10 percent of the people produced services. In the year 2000, labor market projections indicate that only 10 percent of the people working for an income will be making things while 90 percent of the people will produce services.

From 1900 to 2000, in one century, we will have changed from a society where 90 percent of the people produced goods to a society where 90 percent of the people produce services.

Old Grandma doesn't understand that the importance of "old" is that the majority of Americans must now derive their income from producing services. Each year we need fewer people to produce goods. Therefore, we need to create something else for them to do. The American ideal of caring directs them to "produce" services. Because these services are critical in the accounting of our gross national product, we necessarily need more ways of delivering services if our economy is to grow. In an economy primarily based on the production of services, the essential "raw material" is people who are in need or have more needs—people who are deficient.

Just as General Motors needs steel, a service economy *needs* "deficiency," "human problems," and "needs" if it is to grow. It is this economic need that creates a dilemma for Old Grandma, because it demands that we redefine her condition into a problem. This economic need for need creates a demand for redefining conditions as deficiencies.

One amusing example of this "need" is my baldness. Old Grandma thinks that is a condition. Nonetheless, there are an increasing number of caring service deliverers who are trying to persuade me that my baldness is a problem, and recently, a disease.

We see a much more serious expression of the economic need for need in the professional view of women. Old Grandma thought that childbearing and menopause were conditions of womanhood. Professionals have now redefined these conditions as problems to be treated like a sickness.

Another example is children who are too energetic for most people to tolerate. Old Grandma would say, "That child has the energy of two people. She needs a lot of room!" In contrast, the needs of our caring economy take that child's energy and convert it into raw material for more service delivery by calling her hyperactive.

More and more conditions of human beings are being converted into problems in order to provide jobs for people who are forced to derive their income by purporting to deliver a service. This relentless need for income through caring has resulted in a massive new breakthrough during the last half of the twentieth century. During that era we made a great "advance" by redefining two conditions as problems: childhood and aging—the young and the old.

Much of America's post–World War II economy has depended upon redefining the old and young as categories of deficiency and need in order to provide the raw material for income-producing service systems supporting those of middle years. The old and the young have been the gold mines of this society because they are now producing the "natural resource" that so many of us depend upon for our income and our nation depends upon to keep the GNP expanding.

The process by which we create problems based upon age may be best understood if we look first at the *deficiency category* called childhood. In a superb social history called *Centuries of Childhood*, Phillip Aries describes how we have thought about people called children throughout history. He suggests that about 150 years ago, the idea of "childhood" was invented. Prior to that time, centuries of humanity didn't know there was something called "childhood."

Once we had "invented" childhood we could produce a series of institutions and programs to deal with this age classification of people. Before we had childhood, there were terrible things done to children. Modern childhood allowed us to provide young people with caring pediatricians, teachers, recreation programmers, truant officers, sugar-coated breakfast food marketers, counselors, and reformatory guards. This "new class" of caring people needs childhood for their income. As their numbers increase, they develop professional and union organizations with the power to define more and more deficiency among the young. Each new "youth deficiency," called a need, has limited the productivity and the creativity of those people who are assigned to childhood. This economic need for childhood has created "children" who are now benevolently programmed, directed, and controlled people. Through the invention of childhood, we have made them the raw material of "helping" professions. The result has been the loss of the capacity of families, communities, neighbors, neighborhoods, churches, and synagogues to have *children* as a useful part of their communities.

Today, we are paying a terrible price for childhood. We now know the crippling consequences of an age classification called childhood. Nonetheless, our need for more service income is inventing another age classification called "oldhood."

The economic use of classifying "oldhood" as a problem serves two purposes. The first is that it produces more service jobs by classifying old people as problems. Second, by the very act of classification it also defines old people as less productive or nonproductive and diminishes their capacity to compete for jobs. Thus, we create more jobs for one class by diminishing the job capacity of another. Indeed, one might say that what has happened in the United States since World War II is that those people of middle years have needed "problems" called old and young in order to create more "needs" while diminishing the number of people eligible to meet the needs.

As our caring society *needs* to create more income and "productivity," professionally defined oldness and youngness must grow. At Northwestern University, where I work, 83 percent of the people who receive undergraduate degrees now eventually go on for at least two more years of education. Their "childhood" is extended to at least twenty-three years before we declare them useful. For those who are old, useless retirement is being declared to be necessary at an earlier age. The productive years narrow as the "valuable deficiencies" of age-classified uselessness expand.

There is a driving *need* for more oldhood and childhood in our economy. The human impact of the economic need to care is the great peril facing the Old Grandmas of this world. Indeed, Old Grandma persists as old because she will not become a client of the oldhood industry. She will not become a "need," a "problem," or a "deficiency." She insists on being old in spite of the professional and national need for her oldness.

The primary "need" facing Old Grandma is whether she can

survive our economic need for her oldhood. When we hold professional conferences called "New Frontiers of Aging: Life Extension," we are clearly about the commodification of age. We are creating an oldness industry dependent upon "oldhood." It is a very sad "business," making people of age into clients, consumers, and commodities because we *need* oldhood.

There is another way. It requires us to recognize that "old" is more important than the *need* for oldness. For many people in our society, old is a tragedy. For millions of people like Old Grandma, the critical question is not adequate "service." It is a decent income and the care of their kin and neighbors.

If those who wish to "serve" old people want to deal with a real problem, they might consider the fact that in 1950, for every six people who were receiving Social Security, a hundred people were paid workers. By the year 2030, when people who are now thirty years old will be sixty-five, present projections indicate that for every person receiving Social Security there will be two people who are working for an income.

When there are two paid working people for every person receiving Social Security, there will be a critical political problem for "old." Indeed, we are already seeing its ramifications in the current Social Security funding crisis. As more and more people are defined as old and unproductive in the society, what will happen to our desire to provide them a decent income? When every two paid working people must support a third person defined as unproductive because they are old, we can predict a negative political reaction. It will no longer be the welfare recipients who will be seen as a "burden." Instead, it will be a new "burden"—Old Grandma. That is the *real* problem for people who care about old.

This problem may create a great opportunity. We may see a movement to redefine old as productive. It is clear that the oldhood industry will grow as long as old is profitable. Nonetheless, as our society creates too many old consumers and not enough middle-years producers, the political and economic equation may begin to shift. Therefore, for those who seriously care about old, the critical question may be how to allow the old to be productive and valued.

For those who are involved in research regarding old as a deficiency, we should declare a moratorium. Instead, we should ask them to focus upon efforts to define the competence, the skills, and the capacities of old. Perhaps they could use their need to serve to develop understandings that would allow the capacities of old to be valued.

Unfortunately, if we declare a moratorium on research defining old people as "deficient" and in "need" of professional service, we will create an economic crisis among those who *need* the oldhood industry for their income. What will we do with all the professionals, bureaucrats, and working people who now live off "old" defined as unproductive, deficient, and of no value? What will they do to make a living?

Perhaps they could use their hands to make solar energy units on the tops of our houses. Perhaps they could do the work needed to conserve and rebuild our city neighborhoods rather than providing "services" that are needed because our communities have decayed.

If this work is too menial, perhaps the displaced persons in the oldhood industry could be paid for taking care of their parents.

We cannot afford the oldhood industry because it disables Old Grandma. Instead, we need a genuinely anti-age policy. Policies that use age to separate people into the three categories of youth, middle age, and old in order to meet the *needs* of a growth-oriented caring economy should be systematically dismantled. The age-oriented service industries break families, neighborhoods, and community and decimate the caring capacities of human beings.

The ageist oldhood industries and the public policies that support them have created a problem for Old Grandma and my family. Soon, Old Grandma will not be able to live alone in her apartment. If I respond to the incentives of the public policies established by the oldhood industry, the easiest economic choice for me will be to store Old Grandma away in a room in a "geriatric center."

If I want to care for Old Grandma and bring her to my home, all the economics are against me because I am *competing* with the powerful oldhood industry. I am only one person with one vote. The powerful oldness industry needs Old Grandma. They have a lobby. I have none. My care is of *no value* in our GNP just as Old Grandma's old is of no value in the GNP. But Old Grandma is of *great* value to a nation that lives off old as a deficient, incompetent group in need of professional service.

Our current oldhood policy makes it clear to me that the most costly thing I can do is to care enough for Old Grandma that I will bring her to my home when she cannot live alone. The power of the oldhood industry and its public policies is so strong that my family economy will suffer if I care enough about Old Grandma to care for her in my home. Our national policy regarding Old Grandma is anticaring, antifamily, anti-old.

Old Grandma has warned me not to glorify old. Old hurts, like all the rest of life. Old hurts especially because death is near. To be old, you have to face death. The possibility of old as a category of useful life finally depends upon how we view death. If our society's central focus on old is conferences on life extension, *we will create oldhood*. A death-fearing association with old creates the basic incentives for much of the oldhood industry.

Death is a reality. The oldhood industry creates the incentives for a flight from that reality. Indeed, the fear of death is the fuel for much of the oldhood industry.

Old Grandma says she is prepared to die. Nobody "helped" her to be ready. Indeed, she is ready because she grew up when death was not a "problem" but a condition. She was not subjected to the death-denying values of the "life extenders" in the oldness industry and the media glorifiers of youth. She is fortunate. Her old has the power to meet death instead of placing herself in the hands of those who make life extension their commodity and say, "Leave the dying to us."

A 1976 study in a Chicago neighborhood examined the cause of death recorded on death certificates in 1900 and 1975. In 1975, the death certificates said most people died of heart disease, stroke, and cancer. In 1900, the death certificates said the majority of the people died of old age.

When our death certificates once again say that most people die of old age, it will be a good indicator that we have liberated ourselves from the oldhood industry. If we can live with death, we can focus on how "old" can be a valued celebration of our capacities and our mortality.

This chapter is a report of what Old Grandma taught me. I am sharing it with you because it is the most *valuable* thing I know. Its value will not appear in the gross national product because Old Grandma's old is too valuable to be counted by a society that *needs* oldness as a commodity.

Professionalized Service
and Disabling Help

The business of modern society is service. Social service in modern society is business.

This fact is reflected in the language employed. Professionals and their managers now speak of educational "products," health "consumers," and a legal "industry." Clients are defined as "markets," and technocrats—an entirely new breed of professionals—are developing methods to "market" services, using business accounting systems. Computers measure and store psychological "inputs" and family "outputs." There are "units served" and "units of service," and sophisticated economists, statisticians, and planners deal with the production and consumption of social services in the same way as the production, consumption, and maintenance of physical goods is accounted for. Furthermore, and this is of central importance, every modernized society, whether socialist or capitalist, is marked by the growing percentage of service in its gross national product, not only of services such as postal deliveries, catering, and car repairs, but social services such as marriage guidance, birth control counseling, education, legal arbitration, care of the young, the adult, and the old in all its ramifications, and all that falls under the general heading of social help.

This stage of economic development is distinguished by its unlimited potential, since service production has none of the limits imposed by goods production—limits such as natural resources, capital, and land. Therefore, the social service business has endless possibilities for expansion, as there seems to be no end to the needs for which services can be manufactured.

Modernized nations are therefore best defined as service economies. They are serviced societies and they are peopled with service producers and service consumers—professionals and clients.

The politics of serviced societies are gradually being clarified. Public budgets are becoming strained under the service load. Many national and local governments find themselves involved in the unprecedented politics of deciding between competing services—should we give more to education and less to medicine? Within the service sectors there are equally difficult dilemmas. Should we cut back on tax-paid abortions or should the available money be used for free flu vaccine?

These dilemmas are often resolved by the apolitical ideology of service. While old-fashioned politics, rooted in a goods economy, allowed a civic debate as to whether a nation needed more wheat or more steel, more automobiles or more houses, the new service politics is a debate as to whether we should have more doctors or more teachers, more lawyers or more social workers. Politically the question becomes whether we should trade health for learning, or justice for family well-being. These choices create an impossible politics in traditional terms.

While our political traditions make it possible to decide between wheat and steel, it seems politically impossible to decide between health and education because health and education are not alternatives amenable to choices, they are services. Indeed, the allocation of services is so immune to political debate that many governments resolve the dilemma by deciding that we will have less wheat and more education, less steel and more medicine.

This is not to suggest that these choices are correct or incorrect, or even that they define appropriateness. Rather, it is to say that the apolitical nature of service is so pervasive that it is difficult for the public and policymakers to recognize that the creation and allocation of services are the central political issue in many modernized economies.

The political immunity of the services is best understood in terms of the symbolic referent of service:

Services are something one pays for.

The "good" that is paid for is care.

Care is an act that is an expression of love. We say "I care for her more than anyone" or "I am taking care of my mother and father."

Thus, *service* is to *care* which is to *love* and love is the universal, apolitical value.

Symbolically, then, the apolitical nature of service depends on its association with the unlimited universality of love. Ask any servicer what is ultimately satisfying about his work and the answer will most commonly be framed in terms of wanting to care for and help people. Press on and the answer is usually that the individual "loves people."

Since love is not a political issue, care is not a policy question and service becomes the one business that is an unlimited, unquestionable, and nonpolitical "good."

While this analysis may seem overly symbolic, consider the political use of the language of social service in the United States. When the first major program to provide governmentally insured medicine was proposed, it was not described as a policy to expand access to and income for the medical system. It was called Medi*care*.

The president of the American Federation of Teachers noted in an address that there are thousands of unemployed teachers and a large new supply graduating from teacher training institutions. He dealt with the economic dilemma by noting that large sectors of the society need education—the preschool, adult, and elderly populations. In order to meet this "need," he called for a new government program to guarantee the lifelong educational rights of all Americans. He called it Edu*care*.

In the law schools of the United States, law students number 40 percent of all the practicing lawyers in the country. A recent study asked the leaders of the American bar what they thought could be done to ensure that this flood of new lawyers could provide their service and have an adequate income. The most common response was to suggest the need for a publicly supported program that would guarantee the rights of all people to legal services. The name that was universally applied to such a program was Judi*care*.

It is clear, therefore, that the word "care" is a potent political symbol. What is not so clear is that its use masks the political interests of servicers. This fact is further obscured by the symbolic link between care and love. The result is that the politico-economic issues of service are hidden behind the mask of love.

Behind that mask is simply the servicer, his systems, techniques, and technologies—a business in need of markets, an economy seeking new growth potential, professionals in need of an income.

It is crucial that we understand that this mask of service is *not* a false face. The power of the ideology of service is demonstrated by the fact that most servicers cannot distinguish the mask from their own face. The service ideology is *not* hypocritical because hypocrisy is the false pretense of a desirable goal. The modernized servicer believes in his care and love, perhaps even more than in the services. The mask is the face. The service ideology is *not* conspiratorial. A conspiracy is a group decision to create an exploitative result. The modernized servicer honestly joins his fellows to create a supposedly beneficial result. The masks are the faces.

In order to distinguish the mask and the face it is necessary to consider another symbol—need.

We say love is a need. Care is a need. Service is a need. Servicers meet needs. People are collections of needs. Society has needs. The economy should be organized to meet needs.

In a modernized society where the major business is service, the political reality is that the central "need" is an adequate income for professional servicers and the economic growth they portend. The masks of love and care obscure this reality so that the public cannot recognize the professionalized interests that manufacture needs in order to rationalize a service economy. Medicare, Educare, Judicare, Socialcare, and Psychocare are portrayed as systems to meet need rather than programs to meet the needs of servicers and the economies they support.

Removing the mask of love shows us the face of servicers who *need* income, and an economic system that *needs* growth. Within this framework, the client is less a person in need than a person who is needed. In business terms, the client is less the consumer than the raw material for the servicing system. In management terms, the client becomes both the output and the input. His essential function is to meet the needs of servicers, the servicing system, and the national economy. The central political issue becomes the servicers' capacity to manufacture needs in order to expand the economy of the servicing system.

Within this analytical framework, pejoratives are inappropriate. After all, a serviced society provides an economy, a structure for social organization, and service workers motivated by the ethical values of care and love. If these service system needs are legitimate, clients can be viewed as needed, rather than in need, and we can get on with the business of researching, developing, manufacturing, and marketing services without the necessity to project professional need upon citizens. We can deal in political and economic terms with the needs of servicers, freed of the apolitical mask of love.

The problem with this political resolution is political reality. Throughout modernized societies a troublesome question is being raised by the citizenry. In popular terms, it is:

> Why are we putting so much resource into medicine while it is not improving our health?
> Why are we putting so much resource into education and our children seem to be learning less?

Why are we putting so much resource into criminal justice
systems and society seems less just and less secure?

Why are we putting so much more resource into mental
health systems and we seem to have more mental illness?

As if these questions were not troubling enough, a new
group of service system critics are asking whether we are
putting more resources in and getting out the very opposite
of what the system is designed to "produce." In medicine,
this question is most clearly defined as iatrogenesis—doctor-
created disease. The new critics' question is not whether we
get less service for more resources. Rather, it is whether we get
the reverse of what the service system is supposed to "produce." In the terms of Ivan Illich, the question is whether the
systems have become counterproductive. Do we get more sickness from more medicine? Do we get more injustice and crime
with more lawyers and police? Do we get more ignorance with
more teachers and schools? Do we get more family collapse
with more social workers?

This is the question that is most threatening to the previously apolitical service systems, because while services defined
as embodiments of care and love are a political platform; while
services that are understood as being less effective than they
have been in the past are a political possibility; while it is even
politically feasible to remove the mask of love and recognize
services as systems in need of resources in order that
economies may grow, it is politically *impossible* to maintain a
service economy if the populace perceives that the service system hurts more than it helps—that professionalized service can
become disabling help.

In the last few years, the progressive leaders of the service
business have recognized the counterproductive threat. Their
response has been to develop new strategies to deal with the
counterproductivity of service systems. They have called upon
the skills of another profession—the managers. Their assump-

tion is that although professional servicers are unable to control the harm they induce, the managerial profession can become the modern reformer, controlling and directing the systems so that counterproductivity is neutralized, while at the same time protecting the political support for the growth of the service system.

The new service manager, translating his skills from the goods production sector, sees four elements to be manipulated in rationalizing the service system: budgets, personnel, organizational structure, and technology. Therefore, the service manager is now busily at work instituting cost-control systems, developing personnel-training systems, restructuring delivery systems, and introducing new technologies.

The most progressive managers have used their advanced marketing skills to develop a fifth manipulation—preparing the client. They recognize that if there is no need for service, it is possible to manufacture a need. If the popular perceptions of need do not fit the service, social service managers have developed techniques that can persuade people to fit the service through advanced marketing systems.

Will these professional management techniques stabilize the service business by eliminating counterproductive effects? Certainly the capacities of modern management systems are impressive. Aided by the apolitical ideology of the services, one might well prophesy a collaboration between the servicers and their managers to coalesce into an irresistible force that will henceforth direct the economic policies of modernized economies.

An alternative view suggests that there may be an immovable object that faces the irresistible force: a new ideology that assigns to the state the coordination of total disservice.

If such an object exists, it is found in the human necessity to act rather than be acted upon; to be citizen rather than client. It is this human imperative that suggests that even the best-managed service systems will be unable to overcome popular recognition of the disabling impacts of modernized professional service.

The remainder of this chapter attempts to identify the disabling effects of modernized service systems and to suggest the political consequences of the conflict between the irresistible force of client-making and the immovable object of citizen action.

Professionalized Assumptions Regarding Need

Three disabling effects grow from professionalized assumptions of need.

First is the translation of a need into a deficiency. A need could be understood as a condition, a want, a right, an obligation of another, an illusion, or an unresolvable problem. Professional practice consistently defines a need as an unfortunate absence or emptiness in another.

One is reminded of the child's riddle asking someone to describe a glass that has water in its lower half. Is it half-full—or half-empty? The basic function of modernized professionalism is to legitimize human beings whose capacity is to see their neighbor as half-empty. Professionalized research increasingly devotes its efforts to extending the upper rim of the glass in order to ensure that it will never be filled—even by the results of "effective service."

In a servicing economy where the majority of the people derive their income from professionalized "helping" and GNP is measured by services rendered, nations need an increased *supply* of personal deficiency. Thus, a society that purports to meet need defined as personal deficiency is more accurately understood as an economy in need of need. The comic distortion could be societies of neighbors whose income depends upon finding the deficiency in each other. The political consequence is neighbors unable to act as communities of competence with the capacity to perceive or act upon solvable problems.

The *second* disabling characteristic of professionalized definitions of need is the professional practice of placing the perceived deficiency *in* the client. While most modernized professionals will agree that individual problems develop in a socioeconomic-political context, their common remedial practice isolates the individual from the context. The effect of this individualization leads the professional to distort even his own contextual understanding. Because his remedial tools and techniques are usually limited to individualized interaction, the interpretation of the need necessarily becomes individualized. The tool defines the problem rather than the problem defining the tool.

A study of children who became state wards exemplifies the process. The children were legally separated from their families because the parents were judged to be unable to provide adequate care for the children. Therefore, the children were placed in professional service institutions. However, the majority of the professional case records portrayed the children as the problem. Quite correctly, officials who were involved in removing the children from their homes agreed that a common reason for removal was the economic poverty of the family. Obviously, they had no resources to deal with poverty. But there were many resources for professionalized institutional service. The service system met the economic need by institutionalizing an individualized definition of the problem. The negative side effect was that the poverty of the families was intensified by the resources consumed by the "caring" professional services. In counterproductive terms, the servicing system "produced" broken families.

The individualizing, therapeutic definition of need has met a counteracting force in some of the "liberation" movements. The civil rights and women's liberation movements are cases in point. Their essential ideological function is to persuade minorities and women that they are human beings who are neither deficient nor dependent upon systems purporting to meet their "needs" through individualized professional help. Instead, these movements struggle to overcome the individualized-deficiency-oriented "consciousness" communicated by the professional service ideology by affirming individual competence and collective action.

The *third* disabling effect of professionalized definitions of need results from specialization—the major "product" of advanced systems of technique and technology. We all know that this process creates highly specialized, intricately organized service systems that provide magnificent organizational problems for the new service managers. Vast human and financial resources are now devoted to the rationalization of these systems, providing politically acceptable criteria justifying economic growth through the service sector.

What is less clearly understood is that these systems impose their mirror image on the citizenry. As the systems are a set of managed parts, so the client is necessarily understood and processed as a set of manageable parts, each with its own service mechanic. These complex service systems remind one of those table mats in some restaurants that show a cow divided into parts locating the steak, the roast, the ribs, and the tongue.

In like manner, professionalized service definitions increasingly translate need in terms of people in pieces. We need podiatrists for our hooves and eye, ear, nose, and throat men for our snouts. Our psyche, marriage, relationship with our children, in fact our most intimate and personal activities are divided into separate bits and pieces.

Modernized professions also piece us out in time. Service professionals now assure us that we live through a set of needs defined by age. Professionals have "found" seven life crises (formerly known as the seven ages of man) from infancy to death, each requiring its helping professional. Elizabeth Kübler-Ross has advanced the process by giving us five phases of death. Her work ensures a new set of helpers for stage one of dying, stage two of dying, and so on. Following these dying therapists will be research professionals attempting to decide why some people skip, say, stage two or three of dying.

While individualizing need may disable by removing people from the social context, the compartmentalization of the person removes even the potential for individual action. People are, instead, a set of pieces in need, in both time and space. One hopes that the pieces can be put together again to make a human unit of sufficient residual effectiveness to pay for "its" servicing.

To sum up, professionalized services define need as a deficiency and at the same time individualize and compartmentalize the deficient components. The service systems communicate three propositions to the client:

- You are deficient.
- You are the problem.
- You have a collection of problems.

In terms of the interest of service systems and their *needs*, the propositions become:

- We *need* deficiency.
- The economic unit we *need* is individuals.
- The productive economic unit we *need* is an individual with multiple deficiencies.

The Professionalized Assumptions
Regarding the Remedy of Need

These professionalized definitions of need produce a logical and necessary set of remedial assumptions, each with its own intrinsically disabling effects.

The *first* of these assumptions is the mirror image of the individualized definition of need. As *you* are the problem, the assumption is that *I*, the professional servicer, *am the answer. You* are not the answer. *Your peers* are not the answer. *The political, social, and economic environment* is not the answer. Nor is it possible that there is no answer. I, the professional, am the answer. The central assumption is that service is a unilateral process. I, the professional, produce. You, the client, consume.

There are, of course, an impressive set of professionalized coping mechanisms that have been developed by sensitive servicers to deny the unilateral nature of professionalized service. They are described as group-oriented services, peer-oriented services, client-oriented services, and community-oriented services. Each of these rhetorical devices is a symbolic attempt to deal with the anxieties of servicers who *need* to deny the unilateral nature of their relationships.

While it is clear that many humanistic professionals seek a democratic definition for their role, it is difficult to perceive the bilateral component beyond the clients' payment, whether out of pocket or through taxation. Indeed, a basic definition of "unprofessional conduct" is "becoming involved with the client." To be professional is to distance—to ensure that the relationship is defined in terms that allow the client to understand who is *really* being serviced.

In spite of the democratic pretense, the disabling function of unilateral professional help is the hidden assumption that "you will be better because I, the professional, know better."

The political implications of this assumption are central to antidemocratic systems. Indeed, it is possible that societies dependent on economies of unilateral professional servicing are systematically preparing their people for antidemocratic leaders who can capitalize upon the dependencies created by expert, professionalized helpers, who teach people that "they will be better because we, the professional helpers, know better."

A *second* disabling characteristic of professionalized remedial assumptions is the necessity for the remedy to define the need. As professionalized service systems create more elegant techniques and magnificent tools, they create an imperative demanding their use.

The problem with these beautiful, shiny, complex, professional tools and techniques is that their "benefits" are not easily comprehended by the public. We see the professions developing internal logics and public marketing systems that assure use of the tools and techniques by assuming that the client doesn't understand what he needs. Therefore, if the client is to have the benefit of the professional remedy, he must also understand that the professional not only knows what he needs but also knows how the need is to be met.

Thus the complex professional remedial tools have come to justify the professional power to define the need—to decide not only the appropriate remedy but the definition of the problem itself. Increasingly, professions assume that in order to deal with deficiency, they must have the prerogative to decide what is deficient.

There is no greater power than the right to define the question. From that right flows a set of necessary answers. If the servicer can effectively assert the right to define the appropriate question, he has the power to determine the need of his neighbor rather than to meet his neighbor's need.

While this power allows the professional to use his shiny new remedy, it also defines citizens as people who can't understand whether they have a problem—much less what should be done about it.

Modernized societies are now replete with need-defining research. Professionals have recently "discovered" tool-using needs called child abuse, learning disabilities, and "removal trauma" (the need for therapy for children who are traumatized because they are removed from their allegedly traumatic families). Brigitte Berger suggests, in a recent article, that baldness will soon be defined as a disease because underemployed dermatologists will decree it to be one. The final institutionalization of the process is a new program developed by a famous clinic in the United States: the program provides a costly opportunity for people who don't feel anything is wrong to find out what problems they have that meet the needs of new tools.

When the capacity to define the problem becomes a professional prerogative, citizens no longer exist. The prerogative removes the citizen as problem-definer, much less problem-solver. It translates political functions into technical and technological problems.

Once the service professional can define remedy and need, a

third disabling remedial practice develops. It is the coding of the problem and the solution into languages that are incomprehensible to citizens.

While it is clearly disabling to be told you can't decide whether you have a problem and how it can be dealt with, the professional imperative compounds the dilemma by demonstrating that you couldn't understand the problem or the solution anyway. The language of modernized professional services mystifies both problem and solution so that citizen evaluation becomes impossible. The only people "competent" to decide whether the servicing process has any merit are professional peers, each affirming the basic assumptions of the other.

While there are fascinating interjurisdictional disputes among servicing peers, these conflicts rarely break the rule that it is only the professional who understands the problem and the solution. The internal conflicts are power struggles over which professionals shall be dominant. A professional who breaks the rule of professional dominance will be stigmatized by all the disputants and lose his place on the rungs of the ladder to success. The politics of modernized professional power are bounded by peer review. Modern heretics are those professional practitioners who support citizen competence and convert their profession into an understandable trade under the comprehensible command of citizens.

The critical disabling effect of professional coding is its impact upon citizen capacities to deal with cause and effect. If I cannot understand the question or the answer—the need or the remedy—I exist at the sufferance of expert systems. My world is not a place where I do or act with others. Rather, it is a mysterious place, a strange land beyond my comprehension or control. It is understood only by professionals who know *how* it works, *what* I need, and *how* my need is met. I am the object rather than the actor. My life and our society are technical problems rather than political systems.

As the service professions gain the power to unilaterally define remedy and need and to code the service process, a *fourth* disabling characteristic develops. It is the capacity of servicers to define the output of their service in accordance with their own satisfaction with the result. This fourth capacity develops in a service professional just as the citizen is totally and definitely transmogrified into a *critical* addict.

Increasingly, professionals are claiming the power to decide whether their "help" is effective. The important, valued, and evaluated outcome of service is the professional's assessment of his own efficacy. The client is viewed as a deficient person, unable to know whether he has been helped.

This developing professional premise is contested by the consumer movement. The movement is a valiant last stand of those disabled citizens who lay final claim to the right to evaluate the effects or "outputs" of professionalized service.

The basic assumption of the movement is that citizens are enabled because they have become powerful consumers. In this assumption the movement is a handmaiden of the serviced society. It implicitly accepts the service ideology. Citizens *are* as they consume. Citizen welfare is defined by equitable, efficacious consumption. The service system is a given good. The citizen role is in evaluating the output. While citizens may not understand the service system, the consumer movement assumes they do know whether the system's output helps or hurts.

Professionally managed service systems are now dealing with this remnant citizen role as a consumer. The result has been an increasing professional focus on manipulating consumer perceptions of outcomes. Thomas Dewar, in an article titled "The Professionalization of the Client," describes how the service systems are training citizens to understand that their satisfaction is derived from being effective clients rather than people whose problems are solved.

The paradigm of this process is the school. Unlike most servicing systems, the school is transparent in its institutional definition of the client's role. The school client is evaluated in terms of his ability to satisfy the teacher. The explicit outcome of the system is professional approval of behavior and performance.

The professional imperative is now universalizing the ideology of the school, communicating the value of effective clienthood. Negating even the client "output" evaluation, modernized professional services increasingly communicate the value of being an effective client as the proof of the system's efficacy.

Once effective "clienthood" becomes a central value in society, the consumer movement as we know it now will be stifled and will wither away.

The service ideology will be consummated when citizens believe that they cannot know whether they have a need, cannot know what the remedy is, cannot understand the process that purports to meet the need or remedy, and cannot even know whether the need is met unless professionals express satisfaction. The ultimate sign of a serviced society is a professional saying, "I'm so pleased by what you've done." The demise of citizenship is to respond, "Thank you."

We will have reached the apogee of the modernized service society when the professionals can say to the citizen:

- We are the solution to your problem.
- We know what problem you have.
- You can't understand the problem or the solution.
- Only we can decide whether the solution has dealt with your problem.

Inverted, in terms of the needs of professionalized service systems, these propositions become:

- We *need* to solve your problems.
- We *need* to tell you what they are.
- We *need* to deal with them in our terms.
- We *need* to have you respect our satisfaction with our own work.

The most important research issues in modernized societies involve an understanding of the *needs* of servicers and the mechanics of their systems. These systems are obviously important. They provide incomes for a majority of the people. They support national economies. It is, of course, no secret that they are consistently failing to meet their own goals in spite of magnanimous applications of money and personnel. It is becoming more and more evident that rather than *producing* "services," they are creating sensitive but frustrated professionals, unable to understand why their love, care, and service do not re-form society, much less help individuals to function.

We should, therefore, reorient our research efforts toward the needs of servicers. After all, they are a growing majority of people employed in modernized societies and they are an increasingly sad, alienated class of people in *need* of support, respect, care, and love. Modernized societies *need* to determine how we can help these professionalized servicers while limiting their power to disable the capacities of citizens to perceive and deal with issues in political terms.

And if we cannot do that, we should at least understand the political impact of the disabling nature of professionalized definitions of need and remedy.

Professionalized services communicate a worldview that defines our lives and our societies as a series of technical problems. This technical definition is masked by symbols of care and love that obscure the economic interests of the servicers and the disabling characteristics of their practices.

Medicine

The Medicalization of Politics

The United States was once known as a consumer society because of our predilection toward defining life as the use of goods and services. But during recent decades we have become a society that lives by consuming crises. We have ingested such "unpalatables" as civil rights, ecology, overpopulation, Watergate, energy shortages, inflation, and recession. The popular impression is that in the face of crisis we will digest—if not overcome. There is, however, one crisis that has been with us for a generation, and we still cannot seem to get it down. It is popularly known as the "health care crisis."

There is something refreshing about a nonconsumable crisis. It demonstrates the limits of American ingenuity and ensures some continuity in American life. Grandparents, parents, and children can join in common cause as they reflect upon and complain about their continuing health care problems.

There are compelling reasons why the "health care" crisis has not been consumed. The principal reason is that its consumption would contribute to a revolutionary crisis in American politics. The applicability of this proposition may be peculiarly American. If it applies to other developed societies of the capitalist or socialist world, invidious comparisons are left to the reader.

Prescriptions for Reform

The chronic American "health care crisis" has created an impressive array of palliative reforms. Each ineffective remedy has produced a new prescription. At least six therapies have been administered:

1. *The effort to ensure equal access to medical care.* The government has outlawed racial discrimination, supported all manner of programs to increase the number of "health workers," created incentives for doctors to practice in underdoctored areas, and supported regulatory systems to allocate hospital beds in relationship to "medical need."

2. *The focus on improving the quality of health care.* Increased professionalization and professional review processes have received the support of the state and of many modernized medical practitioners.

3. *An attempt to deal with costs.* Comprehensive prepaid systems, health maintenance organizations, Medicare, Medicaid, and the proposal for a national health insurance program represent efforts to conquer the medical system's growing capacity to consume the gross national product.

4. *The effort to involve "health consumers" in the system.* Here, the government and the medical industry are gradually enabling nonprofessionals to participate in the decision-making processes of the system. A few laypeople are given seats in medical congresses, where they may vote on the future policies of the system.

5. *The increasing concern over ethical issues posed by modern medicine.* Organ transplants, abortion, and life-extension technologies provide new crises and new public and professional policies.

6. *The preventive health care movement.* This reform provides policy alternatives designed to "get at the root of the problem." It calls for continuing check-ups, com-

puterized screening systems, and medical outreach plans tied to public education programs that will enable more people to use the system.

Although these reform efforts have consumed the resources and energies of Americans for more than a generation, the work of Dubos, Fuchs, Illich, and others demonstrates that the recent growth of modern medicine has had very little positive effect upon the health of the American people, insofar as health is measured by morbidity and mortality rates. In the face of the mounting evidence that modernized medicine is irrelevant as a major determinant of health, we have responded with phenomenal new investments in medicine. In 1993 the Federal Health Care Financing Administration predicted that health care costs will grow 9.2 percent annually to the year 2000, when the costs will be $1.74 trillion, or 18.1 percent of the gross national product.

Medicine's Hegemony

Since these soaring investments in medicine appear to have so little effect upon our health, the basic question is not "How can we reform medicine?" but "*Why* do we invest so heavily in its reform?" The answer may lie in the very fact that the reform increases the hegemony of the therapeutic ideology.

Consider the predictably hegemonic outcomes of the six American reforms:

1. Achieving equal access serves to confirm the value of medicine by broadening the clientele and establishing the legal premise that the right to *consume* medical services is the central "health" issue. "Progressive" litigation seeks to establish "the right to treatment."
2. The guarantee of quality care serves to intensify popular belief that health-care professionals know what health is. The critical issue is to force or entice the professionals to *produce* "it."

3. Cost control ensures not our health but a rationalized guarantee of the medical system's income. The central issue is how to extend the system while lowering or stabilizing the price.

4. Consumer participation co-opts potentially disruptive citizens by providing participation in medicine as a substitute for political action that might affect the critical determinants of physiological ill health.

5. Ethical "reform" could limit medical hegemony by concluding that such issues as abortion and life extension are not medical prerogatives. However, medical professionals have co-opted theologians and clergy by expanding their trade and becoming the counselors for appropriate decisions regarding these problems.

6. "Preventive" medical care systems can make every person a client each day of his life. Medicalized prevention tells us that we need the medical system precisely because we do not perceive a need.

Each reform, therefore, represents a new opportunity for the medical system to expand its influence, scale, and control. It is no wonder that the reform efforts are often generated by medical interests. Indeed, should the American people come to believe that health is basically a political affair and abandon the medicalized reform efforts, the medical system would deflate like a great balloon pricked by the common sense of citizens. The system needs the hot air of reform if it is to continue to inflate.

The System's Political Functions

Despite the utility of reform as an essential process to promote the growth of medicine, it would be totally inaccurate to suggest that medical reform is basically a self-serving mechanism of the medical industry. Its "nonmedical," political effects are now its most important function. Indeed, the reason the "health care crisis" is so nonconsumable is that we cannot afford to digest it because its functions are so critical to the maintenance of the status quo. The political functions of the system are numerous.

First, in any economy that becomes capital-intensive, means of distributing income are needed in order to create new markets and to forestall disruptive unemployment. "Service" systems rationalize alternative means of income distribution. The expansion of the medical system is, in most modernized societies, a primary means of providing income and markets disguised as help.

Second, expanding medical systems require the manufacture of need. As each new need is created, citizens have an increased sense of deficiency and dependence. Indeed, an essential function of professional medical training is to increase the capacity of the trainee to define his or her neighbor as deficient while reducing the capacity of the neighbor to cope.

Third, as physiological health remains stable or diminishes while medical resources increase, political energies are increasingly consumed in the effort to reform the medical system. Next to inflation and recession, "health" insurance is still the major domestic issue on the U.S. political agenda. The consumption of politics through medical reform is a central function of the "crisis."

Fourth, in many countries current research demonstrates that increasing numbers of people use the medical system for reasons that *doctors* say are not physiologically based. In the United States, well over half the "patients" are classified by doctors as not having physiological problems. When doctors are asked why these people visit them, they identify a series of cultural, social, and economic problems. Therefore, their medical "care" is, by the doctor's own definition, a placebo for that action that could address the cultural, social, economic, and political causes of the malady.

Fifth, the growth of medical hegemony provides the training ground for popular acceptance of expertise. As public belief in the need for medically defined service expands, the people act less as *citizens*. They are more accurately defined as *clients*. Clients are people who believe that they are going to be better because someone else knows better. In the United States this training in "clientage" contributed to support for the Vietnam War. Having been trained by professional servicers to believe in professional expertise, American clients waged war by putting their faith in "systems analysts," "international relations experts," and "management authorities." They were given prescriptions for the problem coded in terms of body counts, mini-listening devices, herbicides, and missions. Prepared for professional dependence, they accepted the diagnosis and prescription of a new breed of war-making professionals.

Sixth, the growth-oriented medical system trains people to accept inequity as the price of progress. Indeed, issues of equity and justice can be most effectively co-opted by the belief that the next professional-technological breakthrough will bring health to everyone if we will only invest our resources in professional "help." This "research and development" argument has been a magnificent mechanism to ensure regressive use of efficacious medical resources while preparing people to accept the generalized proposition that inequity is the price of progress.

Seventh, the most important political role of a growth-oriented medical system is its capacity to obliterate any remaining cultural sense of the limits of a technological society. Communicating its commitment to the death of death, the medical system, by its growth, affirms a worldview that places ultimate value in development, exploitation, and conquest. In a society that is decaying because of the unlimited growth of technology and technique, medicine's primary political function is to obscure the cause of our dying.

Reasserting the Possibility of Politics

Viewed in these terms, the essential function of medicine is the medicalization of politics through the propagation of a therapeutic ideology. This ideology, stripped of its mystifying symbols, is a simple triadic credo: (1) The basic problem is you, (2) the resolution of your problem is my professional control, and (3) my control is your help. The essence of the medical ideology is its capacity to hide control behind the magic cloak of therapeutic help. The power of this mystification is so great that the therapeutic ideology is being adopted and adapted by other interests that recognize that their control mechanisms are dangerously overt. Thus, medicine is the paradigm for modernized domination. Indeed, its cultural hegemony is so potent that the very meaning of politics is being redefined.

Politics is interactive—the debate of citizens regarding purpose, value, and power. But medicalized politics is unilateral—the decision of the "helpers" in behalf of the "helped."

Politics is the act of citizens pooling their intelligence to achieve the maximum human good. Medicalized politics is the disavowal of that common intelligence, for it individualizes—by bestowing clienthood and by replacing policy with the placebos of technique and technology.

Politics is the art of the possible—a process that recognizes limits and grapples with the questions of equity imposed by those limits. Medicalized politics is the art of the impossible—the process whereby an unlimited promise is substituted for justice.

Politics is the act of reallocating power. Medicalized politics mystifies the controlling interests so that their power is no longer an issue and the central political question becomes one of increasing the opportunity to be controlled.

Politics is the act of citizens. Medicalized politics is the control of clients. Indeed, as politics is medicalized there is no need for citizens. Those citizens who remain are unobtrusive stumps of a dead idea. If the medicalization of politics is to be perfected, we must continue to invest in medical reform. Identifying new problems in medical terms is essential to the increased hegemony of the therapeutic ideology.

There is, of course, an alternative. It is *not* "curing" a "sick society." Rather, it is the possibility of politics. It is even a mistake to understand reform as the process of limiting medicine, because medicine's hegemony is the central issue in that formulation.

The chief requirement is to restore politics, for we can find no cure in any medical function that is nothing more than a substitute for politics. The central reform is the conversion of clients to citizens.

A political society, peopled by citizens, will certainly find a need for a limited, valuable craft called medicine. That legitimate craft will be the result of whatever remains of modern medicine when our people have healed themselves by rediscovering their citizenship.

Well-Being: The New Threshold
to the Old Medicine

In a paper entitled "An Unhealthy Obsession," published in *Dun's Review* in June 1976, Dr. Lewis Thomas, preeminent medical author and past president of the renowned Memorial Sloan-Kettering Cancer Center, noted that "less than 1% of the US population dies each year and the life expectancy is over 72 years." Thomas says that this is "not at all a discouraging record once you accept the fact of mortality itself." Nonetheless, he notes an obsessive commitment toward medical technology and a growing demand for "health care." It is this demand that Thomas calls an "unhealthy obsession." "The new danger to our well-being," he says, "is in becoming a nation of healthy hypochondriacs, living gingerly, worrying ourselves half to death."

Thomas concludes that we *should* be worrying, but "worrying that our preoccupation with health may be a symptom of copping out, an excuse to recline on a couch, sniffing the air for contaminants, spraying with germicides, while just outside, the whole of society is coming undone."

Clearly, we have become obsessed with health and addicted to medicine. Consider the middle and upper classes. For them, the importance of the tools of modern medicine has largely disappeared. The radical decline in infectious diseases has left much of medicine with such residual responsibilities as repairing the injuries of suburbanites who become battered as a result of their competitions on racquetball courts and highways.

For lower-income people, medicine is not only inappropriate, it is iatrogenically priced. The primary cause of physical malady among the modernized poor is distinctly environmental and obviously unchangeable with medical tools. There is no medical prescription to cure poverty, slums, and polluted air, water, and food. Nonetheless, this reality has not affected the allocation of tremendous public wealth for medical ministrations to the problems of the poor. In New York City, for example, over half of all public and private program dollars specifically designed to assist poor people are spent on providing their medical care. Indeed, only one-third of these "poverty" allocations reach the poor in income, thus assuring their continued poverty, while providing the justification for financing a monumental medical system that has become a monkey on the back of people without an adequate income.

Extending its reach to new jurisdictions, medicine has recently discovered our oldest citizens. As oldness is medicalized, age is fast becoming a disease and death the unfortunate consequence of those without the courage to have their flesh replaced with plastic parts.

Today, modern technological medicine is so peripheral to our health that it is best understood as a tool in search of a use. Mark Twain said, "If your only tool is a hammer, all problems look like nails." We live in great peril because those who command the medical hammer are now using it to make health into a nail. One can hear the hammer's beat growing louder as it medicalizes more and more of everyday life. Indeed, it is now pounding away at anything remotely associated with health, including those activities that were once called "health alternatives"—initiatives to escape the medical model.

It was only a decade or two ago that the idea of health as a condition of life rather than a product of medicine was discovered anew. We began to hear words of well-being such as "wholistic," "fitness," "self-care," "home birth," and "hospice." Unfortunately, these new definitions and alternatives have increasingly been revealed as nails for the medical hammer.

"Wholistic health" is today most often wholistic medicine, creating a new five-in-one professional acting as a doctor, nurse, psychologist, pastor, and herbalist for a single fee.

"Fitness" has often become an opening for the development of sports medicine and doctor-directed exercise centers.

"Self-care" has tended to become the ultimate medicalizer by teaching each of us how to be allopathic autodidacts.

The "home birth" movement has laid the groundwork for hospital "birthing centers." And the "hospice" movement, initiated a decade ago in the United States to wrest death from hospitalized exile, has become inverted so that hospital-based hospices are growing while community hospices atrophy.

How is it that as we open each door to health, at the end of the corridor we find we have reentered the medical chamber? How is it that our health alternatives and redefinitions have so consistently become nails for constructing new additions to the medical mansion?

The reason we have failed to find another way in the name of health is that we have not adequately comprehended the basic structure that guides the modern allopathic medical system. Because our alternatives have not escaped the essential elements of this medical system, we have actually extended that system's hegemony in the name of health alternatives.

The three essential elements of the modern medical system are management, commodification, and curricularization. The possibility of health in a modern society depends, at the very least, upon our ability to free the idea of health from its subordination to managed, commodified, and curricularized activities. Any health "alternative" that is significantly structured by these three elements will necessarily lead to remedicalization.

An examination of each of these elements reveals their inherent opposition to another way called healthfulness. The sign of *management* is a system of hierarchical control that breaks human activity into tiny pieces. Even today, there is no culture that believes health is the result of oligarchic control and fragmented life. How could a method predicated on these values conceivably allow a healthful way?

The sign of *commodification* is the "health consumer." There is, of course, no possibility that health could be consumed. There has never been a "health consumer." Nonetheless, this medically engineered mythical being has entered the fantasy life of modern society and emerged as a client. A client, of course, is the necessary commodity to meet the needs of the medical system. Thus health becomes a new medium for converting citizens into clients who consume the system's commodities in order to achieve well-being.

The sign of *curricularization* is "health education." This is the process by which a culturally defined capacity to cope is disembodied and disordered so that it can be controlled outside the community. Once health is taken to school it can then be managed and commodified. The transmutation of cultural knowledge of healthful coping into a coded lexicon of expert knowledge is the function of the curriculum. This curriculum disorders popular capacity to cope and celebrate, thus closing the essential doorway to healthful ways.

Most of the inventions or traditions that avoid the hammer-power of these three elements of the modern medical system are to be found in popular activities. A few examples suggest some directions toward other ways. While they are not pure examples, they represent the activities of citizens seeking to capture the healthful power to define and to act outside the medical monopoly:

- Two years ago, a group of citizens in the United States formed an organization called The People's Medical Society. The group has two basic goals. The first is to exert popular control over the medical system. The second is to develop information among members that will diminish or prevent contact with the medical system's authoritarian demands. The response has been phenomenal. There are now 77,000 members, with hundreds more joining monthly. The group is tough, clear-eyed, and cheerfully disrespectful in its efforts to *manage* for medicine the minor place that it rightfully deserves in a healthful society.

• In many low-income communities in the United States, publicly financed medical insurance systematically misdirects public wealth from income to the poor to income to medical professionals. In one impoverished community the people have initiated an experiment that *decommodifies* their health by transferring funds budgeted for medical care into activities that involve community action to change the sickening elements in the local environment. The funds' transfer reflects their movement from client to citizen, from commodity to community.

• Throughout modern societies, growing numbers of people have been institutionalized in the name of their health and well-being. In this manner they are disembedded from the culture of community and instituted as students of a *curricularized* system. In several places in the United States, groups of citizens have joined together to bring institutionalized citizens back into the community in a citizen advocacy movement. With amazing deftness, they knit their new friends back into the fabric of popular life.

Each of these initiatives is a citizen effort to release the healthful possibilities of citizenship and community when social space becomes unmanaged, uncommodified, and decurricularized. The result of these efforts will not be an alternative. Rather, their direction is to open a door toward the thousands of other ways that grow when the monopoly of medicalized health is pushed aside.

These groups struggle against a vision of health as the product of specialized technique dominated by a complex control system. This vision is now manifest in both the halls of

Humana and the "Doctor's Fitness Center." It dominates the lives of many Americans both in sickness and in health.

The reason is that this peculiar "health system" is a technological manifestation of the allopathic belief system. Believing that health results from an assault upon internal pathogens by external powers, the allopathic system is designed to create and propel forces into a corrupted body. It is a system designed to intervene, to invade, to penetrate, and to purge. Its theory is based upon counterforce. It is about the power of the external agent. So it is that the system assembles the elements of technology's most forceful tools in order to finally dominate the body and ultimately to replace its corruptible parts. So it is, also, that these tools necessarily force "well-being" into invasion of the being.

A famous medicine maker, Eli Lilly, placed a motto on each of his bottles in the early days: "A drug without side effects is no drug at all." The negative side effects of the medical health system are now manifest. Designed as an invasive theory, the negative effects of the system are best understood as the loss of that it replaces.

First, as described earlier, the system establishes hegemony over "health alternatives," distorting their intentions and outcomes by substituting the method of technological intervention for salubrity.

Second, each historic community is an implicit experiment in well-being. Through stories and friendships, obligations and wisdom, healthful ways are part of everyday life and common knowledge. The "health system" assaults these healthful domains, providing interventions that replace stories with studies, friends with professionals, obligations with fees, and wisdom with technology. Health is a word for life in the commons. Health systems assault the commons as though it were a pathogen.

Third, our life is often possible because of healing. The basic truth is that we heal. My wound heals. This regenerating capacity is the central reality of our vitality. To lose the knowledge of our personal and communal regenerative power is often the cost of the dominance of the health system. And yet that system, with its interventionist power, is fundamentally impotent as a replacement for our healing power.

Fourth, we have not only the vitality of our healing but the capacity to suffer our mortality. This capacity to cope with suffering and finally celebrate our mortality is the foundation of culture. However, health without pain or death is the vision of a system whose tools are chemicals and plastic parts. In exchange for the power to cope and celebrate, we are offered chemically managed versions of therapeutic oblivion. Our person becomes a managed commodity under expert control. The health system finally replaces our very being with its intervention and, in a perfect inversion, there is left to us health without community, commons, vitality, or even mortality.

Health without community, commons, vitality, and mortality is the negative side effect of a monopoly that believes it produces health through managed, commodified, curricularized activity. As these three practices are incorporated into everyday life in the name of health and well-being, we will merely be opening new doors to the medical health system. As we act in common community to nurture and celebrate our vitality and mortality, the possibility of health will emerge.

It is an allegorical truth of our time that the essentially invasive ideology of the medical health system increasingly forces us to make a choice between the interventions of the system and our community, capacity, vitality, and mortality. It is, admittedly, a difficult choice. However, it is an old choice, for in each generation, we are offered new escapes from freedom.

Diagnosis and the Health
of Community

Paradoxically, the growth of consumer societies has seen a decline in the health-giving utility of the consumption of medical services. This phenomena has been documented by such illustrious research scholars as the English epidemiologist Thomas McKeown in *The Role of Medicine: Dream, Mirage or Nemesis*, sociologist Rene Dubos in *The Mirage of Health*, and economist Victor Fuchs in *Who Shall Live*. Each finds, from a different disciplinary focus, that modernized consumer societies experience less and less health return for higher and higher medical investments. Indeed, Fuchs summarizes the research by reporting that "there is no reason to believe that the major health problems of the average American would be significantly alleviated by increases in the number of hospitals or physicians," and he concludes that "the greatest current potential for improving the health of the American people is to be found in what they do and don't do to and for themselves ... and collective decisions affecting pollution and other aspects of the environment."[1]

While it is true that the environment has always been a primary determinant of health status, medicine has offered a remedy without environmental change. It is the truth of our times that that offer is now failing. We are forced to seek improved health through improved environment because the medical alternative is steadily diminishing in efficacy. Nonetheless, Rene Dubos observes that "to ward off disease or recover health, men as a rule find it easier to depend on the healers than to attempt the more difficult task of living wisely."[2]

It is our curious fate, then, to live in a consumer society where our tremendous purchasing power will not buy health from healers. We are, instead, destined to have to seek health by "living wisely." And it is this new search for health that has resulted in the current use of medically unfamiliar words and concepts such as *wholistic, wellness, promotion,* and *community.* They speak not of healers but of attitudes, values, relationships, and environments where it is possible to live wisely.

While it is possible to imagine "wise environments," it is not readily apparent how medical systems, clinics, and professionals are relevant to them. Is there a place for "healers" in the developing world of wellness? Is there a contradiction between the ways of professional systems and the nature of wise, just communities?

Since 1968, the Center for Urban Affairs at Northwestern University has been studying the nature of healthful local communities. These studies have mainly focused upon urban neighborhoods where lower-income people reside. These neighborhoods clearly reflect the outcomes of urban environments where consumer power is minimal. But they also incorporate thousands of innovations and initiatives to develop community capacity, promote wellness, and approach people and place wholistically. In studying these innovative efforts, the Center has attempted to document the nature of the relationships, attitudes, values, and practices that create "wise environments" and the relationship of medical systems and professionals to these local community-building efforts.

These studies suggest four forms of system and professional relationships that have the potential to enhance community capacity and individual well-being.

Reinvestment Practices

A 1984 study determined the number of dollars provided by federal, state, and county sources designated for the low-income residents of Cook County—the county that incorporates the city of Chicago.[3] The study found that a total of $4,851,113,300 was appropriated by these three governments to specifically benefit low-income people. This amount, divided equally among the Cook County residents with incomes below the official poverty line, would have provided a per capita income of $6,200. Thus, a family of three including a mother and two children would theoretically be the beneficiary of $18,600 on a capitation basis. This figure was, at the time, near the median income for a family of that size.

Further analysis of the Cook County data indicated that 35 percent of the total allocation was provided in direct cash benefits to Cook County's low-income people; 65 percent of the allocation for low-income people was provided in the form of services or vouchers for commodities. The medical care system received 38 percent of all the dollars allocated for the benefit of low-income people.

Statistically, the data indicate that on a per capita basis, the family that might have received an $18,600 income would find $7,068 given to the medical system.

As a matter of epidemiological policy, is it healthful to use over one-third of the public income of poor people for healers rather than for wise environments? What would the research of McKeown, Dubos, and Fuchs tell us about this form of public investment? Is it a health-filled policy choice? Does it create wise environments and build healthful communities?

Whatever the answer, it is clear that the medical system is a major, prosperous growth industry receiving heavy public investments that are appropriated for low-income people. While this industry consumes a considerable portion of the wealth of poor people, it also has the potential to reinvest that wealth in these same people. It is this reinvestment relationship that has created healthful community-building relationships between local medical systems and low-income citizens.

A reinvestment policy recognizes that strengthening the local community economy and income of individuals results, in part, from the economic decisions of the medical system. This can occur in at least four ways:

1. Purchasing from local producers and suppliers of goods and services.
2. Hiring residents of the local area.
3. Targeting contracts for goods and services to support creation of new businesses.
4. Investing institutional resources in local financial institutions such as credit unions, co-ops, and community development loan funds.

As medical resources are reinvested in these ways, the economic status of the local community will be strengthened, with the resulting improvement in health status predicted by community-oriented epidemiologists.

Institutional Analysis

In many low-income communities, medical systems, professionals, and enterprises are the centers of greatest wealth. They are also, and consequently, locations of prestige, legitimacy, and authority. They often stand out as the one neighborhood lighthouse that shines as a beacon throughout the city and society.

Because of this unique, authoritative status, they have great potential to become community-building assets by using their institutional auspices. The functions performed by some local medical institutions include:

- *Advocacy*—Joining coalitions of neighborhood groups, medical leaders can lend their weight to local community development efforts. One hospital president, for example, joined a group of local leaders in lobbying federal officials to fund a highway that would spur local economic growth.

- *Convening*—A local medical facility convened leaders of forty neighborhood groups to create a coalition to focus on housing rehabilitation. Because local medical groups deal with so many diverse local interests and leaders, they often are in a unique position to call these groups together to focus on local issues.

- *Economic Power*—Often, local medical systems have economic credibility that other local institutions and organizations do not. One local hospital became the fiscal agent for a newly developing neighborhood economic development corporation. Another used money received as an award for community service to give $1,000 grants to local merchants for street facade improvements.

- *Personnel*—People working in local medical groups have many skills in addition to those related to medical services. The president of one local hospital reports that "We were important [to the local neighborhood groups] as a technical support group. The intelligence of our staff, as accountants, architects, as spokesmen, was put at the community's disposal. We helped the neighborhood organize politically so that it was in a position to bargain for government resources on its own. We haven't got any money of our own, but we're smart and ambitious and we can be a catalyst."

- *Space*—Often, medical facilities have space unused during various times of the day. In overcrowded urban neighborhoods, this space can be a valuable asset. One hospital has a gym that is used as a part of the local school's physical education program and after-school sports activity. Another hospital provides office space for the local Tenant Security Patrol organization.

In all these ways, medical personnel and facilities can invest in local communities. The potential is clear. There is power to advocate, convene, access external resources, and involve personnel and space. This power is a community asset. Its use can be as critical to regenerating healthful community life as medical intervention in the maladies of people who reside in powerless places.

Healthful Information

Medicine has the unintended side effect of mystifying the cause and cure of malady. Many people encounter a life interruption, call it a disease, and take it to a doctor or hospital, where it is treated un-understandably by people who speak in mystifying tongues. The result is for the "person" to become a "patient" in the face of malady. The malady becomes a commodity of the medical profession, and health becomes a consumable as citizens become "health consumers."

Wise communities have the information necessary to avoid becoming frequent consumers of the services of medical industries. And yet it is the coding, commodification, and mystification of the medical industries that is a major barrier to community wisdom. (The next chapter, "Politicizing Health Care," describes a wise community acting upon demystified medical information.) Medical people are, as McKeown, Dubos, and Fuchs remind us, the constant economic beneficiaries of unjust, disorganized, powerless communities. As long as they interpret this fact in terms of their "life-giving" therapies, the communities they "serve" will be misled, weakened, and diseased. However, the translation of medical data into "community-friendly" information is a critical contribution to wise, healthful community life.

Anti-Diagnosis

The obvious center of the medical mentality is the focus upon malady, deficiency, disease, and need—the empty half of the glass. Clearly, the empty half is present. And just as clearly, the full half is present.

The medical system needs the empty half.

The healthful community needs the full half. Indeed, every community has been built by the capacities of needy people and the skills of deficient people. No community was ever built by a group of "full," unneedy, undiseased people. Communities are built in spite of the dilemmas, problems, deficiencies, and diseases of its people.

Nonetheless, potentially powerful communities can be disabled by alien systems that sponsor and propagate a culture of need and deficiency. If this culture of deficiency comes to dominate a local community, it will lose the power of wise citizenship and succumb to the maladies of clienthood and medical consumption.

The essence of the medical mentality is diagnosis—the ability to name and describe the emptiness of your neighbor. As a technique, this skill can be valuable. However, as a pervasive cultural value, it will inevitably blind communities to the capacities, assets, skills, and gifts that are essential to their power, wisdom, and health.

The diagnostic culture is a disease infecting many low-income communities. Its literal manifestation is the "needs survey" that insists that local residents focus upon their emptiness. While this emptiness, deficiency, malady, and disease is *needed* by growing medical systems, it is useless to those who grow healthful communities.

The raw material of community is capacity. The raw material of medicine is deficiency. In this harsh reality is a competition for resources based upon an ideological struggle. The community-building interest is in an antidiagnostic ethos focused on gifts to be manifested. The medical interest is in a prodiagnostic ethos focused upon brokenness to be fixed. Each is a worldview that shapes how power and resources are allocated and which values are affirmed and legitimized. Each creates a map of community that guides community residents, local groups, major institutions, and governments toward competing visions of healthful communities.

The diagnostic ideology creates a community map of needs and deficiencies (Figure 1). This map empowers medical, social, and service systems. It creates a powerful resource magnet. It converts citizens to clients and producers to consumers. It announces to citizens in the community that "you will be better because we know better."

The antidiagnostic ideology creates a map of capacities and assets (Figure 2).[4] This map empowers citizens, associations, and enterprises. It can also create a powerful resource magnet. However, in an era of scarce resources, it must inevitably compete with the prodiagnostic interests.

It is the reality of this competition for the fiscal, political, social, and psychic powers of society that is at the heart of the public health debate and the policy decisions we face.

It would be a hopeful conclusion of this chapter to suggest that there is an obvious synthesis of these two maps—a win-win strategy that enhances both the needs and asset maps. Such a conclusion would be dishonest.

Instead, we should be guided by the critical honesty of Hippocrates, the founder of medicine as a profession. His oath concludes with a mandate to recognize that "above all," medicine's highest value is to "do no harm." In terms of community health, the oath translates into a recognition that an antibody of wise communities is antidiagnosis.

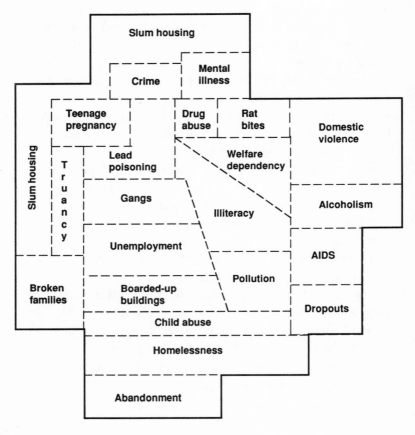

FIGURE 1
Neighborhood Needs Map

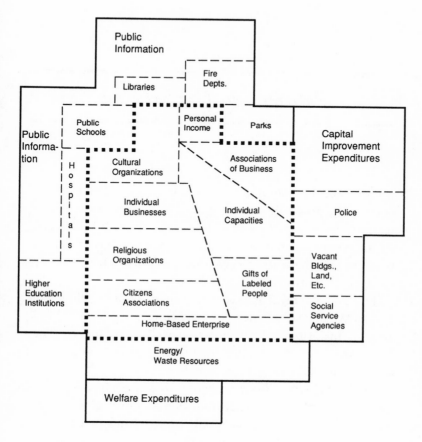

FIGURE 2
Neighborhood Assets Map

Politicizing Health Care

Is it possible that out of the contradictions of medicine one can develop the possibilities of politics? The example I want to describe is not going to create a new social order. It is, however, the beginning of an effort to free people from medical clienthood, so that they can perceive the possibility of being citizens engaged in political action.

The example involves a community of about 60,000 people on the West Side of Chicago. The people are poor and black, and the majority are dependent on welfare payments. They have a voluntary community organization that encompasses an area in which there are two hospitals.

The neighborhood was originally all white. During the sixties it went through a racial transition and over a period of a few years, it became largely populated with black people.

The two hospitals continued to serve the white people who had lived in the neighborhood before the transition, leaving the black people struggling to gain access to the hospitals' services.

This became a political struggle and the community organization finally "captured" the two hospitals. The boards of directors of the hospitals then accepted people from the neighborhood, employed black people on their staffs, and treated members of the neighborhood rather than the previous white clients.

After several years, the community organization felt that it was time to stand back and look at the health status of their community. As a result of their analysis, they found that although they had "captured" the hospitals, there was no significant evidence that the health of the people had changed since they had gained control of the medical services.

The organization then contacted the Center for Urban Affairs, where I work. They asked us to assist in finding out why, if the people controlled the two hospitals, their health was not any better.

It was agreed that the Center would do a study of the hospitals' medical records to see why people were receiving medical care. We took a sample of the emergency room medical records to determine the frequency of the various problems that brought the people into the hospitals.

We found that the seven most common reasons for hospitalization, in order of frequency, were:

1. automobile accidents.
2. interpersonal attacks.
3. accidents (non-auto).
4. bronchial ailments.
5. alcoholism.
6. drug-related problems (medically administered and nonmedically administered).
7. dog bites.

The people from the organization were startled by these findings. The language of medicine is focused upon disease, yet the problems we identified have very little to do with disease. The medicalization of health had led them to believe that "disease" was the problem that hospitals were addressing, but they discovered instead that the hospitals were dealing with many problems that were not diseases. It was an important step in increasing consciousness to recognize that modern medical systems are usually dealing with maladies—social problems—

rather than disease. Maladies and social problems are the domain of citizens and their community organizations.

A Strategy for Health

Having seen the list of maladies, the people from the organization considered what they ought to do, or could do, about them. First of all, as good political strategists, they decided to tackle a problem that they felt they could win. They didn't want to start out and immediately lose. So they went down the list and picked dog bites, which caused about 4 percent of the emergency room visits at an average hospital cost of $185.

How could this problem best be approached? It interested me to see the people in the organization thinking about that problem. The city government has employees who are paid to be "dog-catchers," but the organization did not choose to contact the city. Instead, they said: "Let us see what we can do ourselves." They decided to take a small part of their money and use it for "dog bounties." Through their block clubs they let it be known that for a period of one month, in an area of about a square mile, they would pay a bounty of five dollars for every stray dog that was brought in to the organization or had its location identified so that organizational representatives could go and capture it.

There were packs of wild dogs in the neighborhood that had frightened many people. The children of the neighborhood, on the other hand, thought that catching dogs was a wonderful idea, so they helped to identify them. In one month, 160 of these dogs were captured and cases of dog bites brought to the hospitals decreased.

Two things happened as a result of this success. The people began to learn that their action, rather than the hospital's, determines their health. They were also building their organization by involving the children as community activists.

The second course of action was to deal with something

more difficult—automobile accidents. "How can we do anything if we don't understand where these accidents are taking place?" the people said. They asked us to try to get information that would help to deal with the accident problem, but we found it extremely difficult to find information regarding when, where, and how an accident took place.

We considered going back to the hospitals and looking at the medical records to determine the nature of the accident that brought each injured person to the hospital. If medicine was thought of as a system that was related to the possibilities of community action, it should have been possible. It was not. The medical record did not say, "This person has a malady because she was hit by an automobile at six o'clock in the evening on January 3rd at the corner of Madison and Kedzie." Sometimes the record did not even say that the cause was an automobile accident. Instead, the record simply tells you that the person has a "broken tibia." It is a record system that obscures the community nature of the problem, by focusing on the therapeutic to the exclusion of the primary cause.

We began, therefore, a search of the data systems of macroplanners. Finally we found one macroplanning group that had data regarding the nature of auto accidents in the city. It was data on a complex, computerized system, to be used in macroplanning to facilitate automobile traffic! We persuaded the planners to do a printout that could be used by the neighborhood people for their own action purposes. This had never occurred to them as a use for their information.

The printouts were so complex, however, that the organization could not comprehend them. So we took the numbers and transposed them onto a neighborhood map showing where accidents took place. Where people were injured, we put a blue X. Where people were killed, we put a red X.

We did this for all accidents for a period of three months. There are 60,000 residents living in the neighborhood. In that area, in three months, there were more than 1,000 accidents. From the map the people could see, for example, that within three months six people had been injured and one person killed in an area 60 feet wide. They immediately identified this place as the entrance to a parking lot for a department store. They were then ready to act, rather than be treated, by dealing with the store owner, because information had been "liberated" from its medical and macroplanning captivity.

The experience with the map had two consequences. One, it was an opportunity to invent a way to define a health problem so that the community could understand it. The community organization could then negotiate with the department store owner and force a change in its entrance.

Two, it became very clear that there were accident problems that the community organization could not handle directly. For example, one of the main reasons for many of the accidents was the fact that higher authorities had decided to make several of the streets through the neighborhood major thruways for automobiles going from the heart of the city out to the affluent suburbs. Those who made this trip were a primary cause of injury to the local people. Dealing with this problem is not within the control of people at the neighborhood level, but they understood the necessity of getting other community organizations involved in a similar process, so that together they could assemble enough power to force the authorities to change the policies that serve the interests of those who use the neighborhoods as their freeway.

The third community action activity developed when the people focused on "bronchial problems." They learned that good nutrition was a factor in these problems, and concluded that they did not have enough fresh fruit and vegetables for good nutrition. In the city, particularly in the winter, these foods were too expensive. So could they grow fresh fruit and vegetables themselves? They looked around, but it seemed difficult in the heart of the city. Then several people pointed out that most of their houses are two-story apartments with flat roofs. "Supposing we could build a greenhouse on the roof, couldn't we grow our own fruit and vegetables?" So they built a greenhouse on one of the roofs as an experiment. Then a fascinating thing began to happen.

Originally, the greenhouse was built to deal with a health problem—inadequate nutrition. The greenhouse was a tool, appropriate to the environment, that people could make and use to improve health. Quickly, however, people began to see that the greenhouse was also an economic development tool. It increased their income because they now produced a commodity to use and also to sell.

Then another use for the greenhouse appeared. In the United States, energy costs are extremely high and are a great burden for poor people. One of the main places where people lose (waste) energy is from the rooftops of their houses—so the greenhouse on top of the roof converted the energy loss into an asset. The energy that escaped from the house went into the greenhouse, where heat was needed. The greenhouse, therefore, was an energy conservation tool.

Another use for the greenhouse developed by chance. The community organization owned a retirement home, and one day one of the elderly people discovered the greenhouse. She went to work there and told the other old people, and they started coming to the greenhouse every day to help care for the plants. The administrator of the old people's home noticed that the attitude of the older people changed. They were excited. They had found a function. The greenhouse became a tool to empower older people—to allow discarded people to be productive.

Multility vs. Unitility

The people began to see something about technology that they had not realized before. Here was a simple tool—a greenhouse. It could be built locally and used locally, and among its "outputs" were health, economic development, energy conservation, and enabling older people to be productive. A simple tool requiring minimum "inputs" produced multiple "outputs" with few negative side effects. We called the greenhouse a "multility."

Most tools in a modernized consumer-oriented society are the reverse of the greenhouse. They are systems requiring a complex organization with multiple inputs that produce only a single output. Let me give you an example. If you get bauxite from Jamaica, copper from Chile, rubber from Indonesia, oil from Saudi Arabia, lumber from Canada, and labor from all these countries and process these resources in an American corporation that uses American labor and professional skills to manufacture a commodity, you can produce an electric toothbrush. This tool is what we call a "unitility." It has multiple inputs and one output. However, if a tool is basically a labor-saving device, then the electric toothbrush is an antitool. If you added up all the labor put into producing it, its sum is infinitely more than the labor saved by its use.

The electric toothbrush and the systems for its production are the essence of the technological mistake. The greenhouse is the essence of the technological possibility. The toothbrush (unitility) is a tool that disables capacity and maximizes exploitation. The greenhouse (multility) is a tool that minimizes exploitation and enables community action.

Similarly, the greenhouse is a health tool that creates citizen action and improves health. The hospitalized focus on health disables community capacity by concentrating on therapeutic tools and techniques requiring tremendous inputs, with limited outputs in terms of standard health measures.

Conclusions

Let me draw several conclusions from the health work of the community organization.

First, out of all this activity, it is most important that the

health action process has strengthened a community organization. Health is a political issue. To convert a medical problem
into a political issue is central to health improvement. As our
action has developed the organization's vitality and power, we
have begun the critical health development. Health action
must lead away from dependence on professional tools and
techniques, toward community-building and citizen action.
Effective health action must convert a professional-technical
problem into a political, communal issue.

Second, effective health action identifies what you can do at
the local level with local resources. It must also identify those
external authorities and structures that control the limits of the
community to act in the interest of its health.

Third, health action develops tools for the people's use,
under their own control. To develop these tools may require us
to diminish the resources consumed by the medical system. As
the community organization's health activity becomes more effective, the swollen balloon of medicine should shrink. For example, after the dogs were captured, the hospital lost clients.
Nonetheless, we cannot expect that this action will stop the
medical balloon from growing. The medical system will make
new claims for resources and power, but our action will intensify the contradictions of medicalized definitions of health. We
can now see people saying: "Look, we may have saved $185 in
hospital care for many of the 160 dogs that will not now bite
people. That's a lot of money! But it still stays with that hospital. We want our $185! We want to begin to trade in an econ-
omy in which you don't exchange our action for more medical
service. We need income, not therapy. If we are to act in our
health interest, we will need the resources medicine claims for
its therapeutic purposes in order to diminish our therapeutic
need."

These three principles of community health action suggest
that improved health is basically about moving away from
being "medical consumers."

The experience I have described suggests that the sickness

that we face is the captivity of tools, resources, power, and consciousness by medical "unitilities" that create consumers.

Health is a political question. It requires citizens and communities. The health action process can enable "another health development" by translating medically defined problems and resources into politically actionable community problems.

Human Service Systems

A Nation of Clients?

Futurists are intriguing. They represent one of the newer professions, although in ancient times they might have been called prophets. One of the major functions of futurists is to give us a name for the years ahead—labels like the "postindustrial society," the "cybernetic society," the "society of limits," or the "information society."

Those of us who are not prophets or futurists can use only the tools of mortals to try to understand our prospects. Our best tool is the past, because the past is still the prelude. What each of us knows and has experienced might best predict our future in spite of the futurist's efforts to tell us what we don't know.

What do we know about our history? As a people, Americans love work. We are the people whose work created a new vision of human possibility. We can't stand something that doesn't work.

We measure our very well-being as a society by the product of our work: the gross national product. The gross national product is America's bottom line. If it goes up, America is getting better. If it goes down, America is getting worse. It is the sum of two numbers, the *goods* and the *services* we produce each year.

The gross national product is an unusual number. Consider a day care center and a child care worker interacting with a young child; consider also an automobile factory and a worker putting a windshield wiper on a new automobile. The gross national product adds those two tasks together as though they were the same thing because both are paid work. The same work can also be counted in terms of the number of people who do the work, the number of people who receive money for producing *goods*, and the number who are paid for producing *services*.

Looking back at our history, the work of Americans has changed radically in terms of the number of jobs producing goods and the number producing services. In 1880, about 80 percent of the paid workers produced goods; 20 percent were involved in producing services.[1]

If some of the labor economists' projections are correct, by the year 2000, 90 percent of the paid workers in this country will produce services and 10 percent will produce goods. Thus, our past predicts. In the 120 years between 1880 and 2000, America will have changed from a society in which two out of ten paid workers produced services to one in which nine out of ten paid workers produce services.

Historically, the very nature of human development has been defined by the work that people do and the tools they use: hunters, gatherers, farmers, Bronze Age, Iron Age, and the Industrial Revolution. If we are to label ourselves in these historical terms, we are a people nearing the end of a revolution in work. Indeed, we are *now* living in a new age—the service economy.

As a working people, we are no longer wheat stackers, steel makers, and hog butchers. We are doctors, teachers, clerks, social workers, insurance agents, and bureaucrats.

This shift in the nature of work—the movement to a service economy—may be the most important change that we've experienced in ur century. It is a change that is largely unrecognized, but public welfare workers are the very embodiment of that change. Public welfare workers *are* the service economy. Therefore, it is important that we understand the nature of a service economy if we are to prepare for our future and the future of those we serve.

The Service Economy Expresses the Highest Hope of Human Beings

There are at least six facts about a service economy that are important to people in the public welfare field. First, the service economy is an expression of the highest hopes of human beings. We no longer depend upon the sweat of our brow to survive. We don't have to spend all our lives in the mines, the fields, and the factories. We can care and serve; we are now a society where two-thirds of the people derive their income through service. Thus, the last century has seen the fulfillment of one of the great dreams of humankind.

Second, we need to recognize that the largest institution for producing human services is government.[2] Government or government-funded programs have been the primary instruments for implementing the dream of a service economy. Yet that dream is being threatened across America by the popular tax revolts. Many people are rebelling against the dream by voting to shut off the major sector that produces services. It is a paradox. We dreamed of a society that could serve, but many Americans are now rejecting that dream.

Third—and particularly important for people concerned about the poor—much of the service economy is not place-related. The production of goods—growing wheat or making steel—can best be done in specific places. In the service sector there are fewer limits on the places where work can be done. For example, when I want to travel to Washington, I pick up a telephone in Chicago to make a hotel reservation. The person on the other end of the line asks me where I want to stay. After I say, "Washington," I ask, "Where are you?" She says, "I'm in Memphis." I ask what she is doing. She says, "I'm checking with our computer in New York." So from Chicago to Memphis to New York to Washington I reserve a room.

This phenomenon is characteristic of much of the service economy. There is no particular place that controls where the work is done—unlike a steel mill or a farm. Nonetheless, because we still think in terms of producing goods, we believe that people need to go where the work is. The service economy, however, presents a great opportunity to move work to where people who need work are located. There is no reason that the telephone operator in Memphis has to be in Memphis. She could be on the South Side of Chicago and the system would work just as well. Unfortunately, in most of our great cities, we have put our service industries downtown in the commercial district. As a result of modern technologies there is no reason for them to be there. We ought to be creating the incentives that would locate the jobs of the service economy in neighborhoods where people need work rather than stacking them up in skyscrapers in the center of cities and wasting energy to transport people there.

There is a fourth point about the service economy that is essential to the interest of lower-income people. Most people understand the development of the service economy as a shift from blue-collar to white-collar work. We assume that a white-collar worker needs more education than a blue-collar worker. However, a close look at the nature of the *developing* work in the service economy shows that that assumption is often incorrect. In fact, what is happening now in the service economy is a massive rationalizing and segmenting of work. The same thing that happened to automobile-making on the assembly line is happening to white-collar work.

Think about your own experience. The most visible example of this mass production system applied to service work is the franchise industry. Go to a fast food franchise. You ask the service employee for a hamburger. She turns around and picks out a green-paper-wrapped item marked "hamburger." She then turns to the cash register, which has a green key that says "hamburger." If she can't read "hamburger," she does know green. She punches the button and it shows the price, $0.75. You give her $1.00. She must be educated enough to be able to punch the buttons that ring up $1.00. The machine will subtract $0.75 from $1.00 and tell her your change is $0.25. Anyone who tells you that that woman, because she is in a service industry, needs to be better educated than the person who is working in a steel mill does not understand what is happening in America. Throughout America service work is being "assembly-lined," broken down into small pieces that are within the command of most people who have dropped out of high school.

This industrialization of the service economy means that if we're serious about producing opportunities for people who have been disadvantaged, the service economy is not a system that necessarily demands more education. Indeed, the managers of the service economy are creating a system that often requires *less* education than is needed by a farmer or a steel worker.

Fifth, we need to recognize that there is still a tremendous need for more service jobs. If some labor economists are right, between 1980 and the year 2000 we will have employed 15 to 20 million more people in service occupations.[3] Put in terms of people, that means that we will effectively convert a million goods-producing jobs a year, for twenty years, into service jobs. Perhaps the greatest challenge for those two decades will be deciding what those jobs will be. Today our high schools, junior colleges, and universities are filled with people who expect to deliver services. But what services do we need?

Human Need Is the Raw Material of the Service Economy

This question leads to the sixth point about a service economy. Most of us believe that there is no limit to how much service we can produce. If service is an expression of care, then certainly it is clear that you can never care enough.

We recognize that there is a limit to the goods we can produce because the raw materials are limited. The raw materials of the steel industry are coal, lime, and iron. We know these resources are limited. On the other hand, the raw material of the service economy is human need. Our *deficiencies* and unmet needs are the ore and coal of the service industry. Thus, the servers called teachers need students. But as their raw material declines, as the baby boom drops off, what are they to do? How can they justify their work in the same numbers as the child population decreases? One answer is to "discover" new needs, unperceived needs, unmet needs—or the need for "life-long learning."

Consider American law schools. In the early 1980s alone they produced 127,000 lawyers, increasing by 25 percent the number of licensed attorneys.[4] What is the need—the raw material—for their industry? What will all of these new lawyers say you need that you didn't know you needed?

The service economy presents a dilemma: the *need for need.* As a million people each year move from goods to service production, the service industry requires more raw material— more need. We can now see that "need" requires us to discover more human deficiencies.

I have recently observed two examples of this discovery of new human need. At a conference on service to the elderly, I met a person being trained as a bereavement counselor. She will receive a master's degree in order to help people through their grief after they have lost a loved one—for a fee.

How many people in the United States are feeling that they have a "need" for that bereavement counselor? Certainly people grieve; it is a hurt that people have suffered for eons. But does that grief constitute a need for service? Or does the bereavement counselor need that hurt more than the person in grief needs her help?

Another example is a person I recently met in a Canadian city: He is a recluse manager. This service was developed when a recluse died and no one found him until fourteen days later. A newspaper photographer took a picture of the room where he lived. People were shocked, and the result was the conversion of his death into a need. The local government created a committee of officials that decided to respond to the need his death created. They recommended that the city create a new service—recluse management. The committee also wrote a manual that now guides recluse managers. It tells the managers how to find recluses, how to observe them without their knowing they are being observed, and when to intervene in their lives.

Does the person in grief or the recluse "need" service? Or does the service economy need grief and recluses? Considering the gross national product as an indicator of the national well-being, the answer is clear. If kin deal with grief, it will never be counted as a product. If a bereavement counselor deals with the grief, our gross national product will increase. If an old man dies and is undiscovered for fourteen days, he is worthless. If a recluse manager controls his death, the service economy will count his death as a product of value.

In the city of Chicago, where I work, the neighborhoods are falling down around us. People need work and a decent income. While there is less and less money for the poor, there are more bereavement counselors and recluse managers—more and more servicers who need the poor. We may have reached that point where there are more people in Chicago who derive an income from serving the poor than there are poor people.

Welfare workers are caught in this dilemma. Do they need the welfare clients more than the clients need their service? In a service economy, the welfare recipient is the raw material for case workers, administrators, doctors, lawyers, mental health workers, drug counselors, youth workers, and police officers. Do the servicers need the recipient more than she needs them?

In terms of the gross national product, the answer is clear. The recipient is much more valuable in her dependency; she is a national resource. If she were a productive member of our society, the net loss to the gross national product could be very significant because she may never produce as much income as the income derived from her dependency.

Northwestern University recently completed a study in a

low-income neighborhood where 60 percent of the people are dependent on welfare.[5] In that neighborhood, for every welfare dollar a recipient received in cash income, $0.57 was spent for only one service—medical care. One dollar for the poor and $0.57 for doctors, nurses, and hospitals. Who really needs whom in that kind of economy? Those who provide services for that neighborhood may derive more income from welfare than those who receive welfare. That is not a poor neighborhood; it is a serviced neighborhood.

Institutions and Interests Promote Clienthood and Dependency

There is, of course, another way. We don't have to have policies that produce dependency. Instead, we need policies that recognize the importance of the right to work, the right to income, the right to real authority, the right to care rather than to be served, the right to tools that allow people to produce rather than to consume, the right to working neighborhoods, the right to working farms, and the right to be free from racism. These are the rights we really need—not more service. On the other hand, we must admit that we have failed to identify the enemies of those rights.

My father recently told me that during the New Deal when Franklin Roosevelt was president, most people understood this country as a place where there were *interests* that were the enemies of the common people. But, he said, today we identify the enemy of the people as poverty, sickness, and disease. My father insists that the enemy isn't poverty, sickness, and disease. He argues that the enemy is a set of institutions and interests that are advantaged by clienthood and dependency.

His wisdom reminds us of what we already know. Enemies of the right to work and the right to income are those professionals involved in increasing the demand for certification and licensure of work. Professional efforts to certify work in the service area are stealing jobs away from the poor by putting those jobs in an elite status, requiring the kind of training and education that most poor people do not have.

The enemies of the right to work and the right to income are the business leaders who continue to support and maintain large-scale unemployment and underemployment.

The enemies of the right to authority—the power of people to act and decide—are governmental officials and bureaucrats who are fearful of a transfer of authority. They want "participation" but oppose popular control.

The enemies of the right to popular tools are the technologists who create "megasystems" that provide work for a very few and increasingly produce goods that working people can't afford.

The enemies of the right to working neighborhoods are those banks, savings and loans, and insurance companies that literally steal the savings of poor and working-class people and use that money to make loans to foreign governments to build tanks or to corporations to build resort condominiums in distant states.

The enemies of the farm people are the agribusinesses of America.

The enemies of the "voice of the people" are the great television networks that have created a mindless uniquack that drowns out the voices of the poor as they try to speak to us.

The enemy of freedom from racism is all of us—all of us who have so quickly forgotten Dr. Martin Luther King's dream.

My father, that voice of older America, is right. The enemy is not poverty, sickness, and disease. The enemy is a set of interests that need dependency masked by service.

There is a clear need for public servants—*not* public servicers—and to engage in a new struggle to reinvent America. The incrementalism that we have depended upon just isn't working anymore. We cannot delude ourselves. We must be true to ourselves and to those we represent.

We are in a struggle against clienthood, against servicing the poor. We must reallocate the *power, authority,* and *legitimacy* that have been stolen by the great institutions of our society. We must oppose those interests of governmental, corporate, professional, and managerial America that thrive on the dependency of the American people. We must commit ourselves to reallocation of power to the people we serve so that we no longer will need to serve. Only then will we have a chance to realize the American dream: the right to be a citizen and to create, invent, produce, and care.

Do No Harm

The medical profession has long understood that its interventions have the potential to hurt as well as to help. The Hippocratic oath, repeated by physicians to this day, concludes with the primary mandate, "This above all, do no harm." The harmful capacity of medicine is recognized in what current medical language calls iatrogenic disease—doctor-created maladies.

Much of the positive reputation of the medical profession flows from the ethic that assumes a good doctor, before undertaking any intervention, always asks: "Will this initiative help more than hurt?" Responsible professionals are bound by Hippocrates to consider the balance before acting. Indeed, in the most ethical practice, the burden of proof for efficacy is upon the physician.

The traditional ethical code that prominently displays the Hippocratic principle in the foreground of the medical profession stands in stark contrast to the theory, research, and practice of most other "human service" professions. In the fields of social work, developmental disabilities, physical disability, or care of the elderly, no tradition of routinely analyzing possible negative side effects exists. Instead, evaluation usually focuses on whether an intervention "made a difference." The intervention is presumed to help if it has any effect at all, and if it has no measurable effect, it is assumed not to have hurt.

Some observers suggest the lack of accounting for negative effects in the human services is a consequence of those interventions not being "powerful" ones when compared with the chemicals and scalpels of medicine. Instead, there is an unstated assumption that these nonmedical professions are searching for something that "works" within fields characterized by effective, neutral, or abandoned initiatives, none of which could have basically injured their clients. It is this naive assumption that has degraded the nonmedical human service professions and contributed to popular impressions that many of the clients of these professions are not worth a public investment. Indeed, we now hear the constant claim that the clients of human service professionals—the poor, disadvantaged, disabled, young, and old—have not been helped by "pouring money on the problem."

The client is usually blamed for not blooming under this "rain of dollars." What has actually happened, however, is that money has been "poured" into the programs of human service professionals,[1] and we have no knowledge of whether the effects of their ministrations have been iatrogenic. Instead, the labeled and vulnerable in our society are blamed. From this perspective, the public policies of the last several decades can be understood as an era of blaming the client for many of the iatrogenic practices of human service professionals. Regressive policymakers and human service professionals have made unintended common cause because the profession is unable to analyze the negative effects its interventions have had as the potential cause of failed policy.

If we are to recover the potential of public policy as an asset for those who are labeled, exploited, and excluded, it is critical that we begin to understand the iatrogenic aspects of the major agent of public policy—the human service professions. When we can conceptualize the structurally negative effects of their interventions, we can begin a reasoned decision-making process regarding the two basic questions that should determine social policy:

- "Which of the competing human service solutions have more efficacy than negative side effects?"
- "Is there a less iatrogenic solution that does not involve human service methods?"

This latter question is a critical element of the policymaking process. We often forget that a human service is only one response to a human condition. There are always many other possibilities that do not involve paid experts and therapeutic concepts.

Mark Twain reminds us that "if your only tool is a hammer, all problems look like nails." While the human service tool has undoubted efficacy in particular situations, like the hammer, it can also do great harm when used inappropriately. All the problems of those who are vulnerable, exploited, excluded, or labeled are not nails. They do not always "need" human services. More often, they may "need" justice, income, and community.

This chapter is an attempt to formulate a conceptual framework to assess the iatrogenic effects of the tool called human services. What structurally negative effects does it incorporate? When is it inappropriately used? And what methods might test the iatrogenic potential?

There are at least four structurally negative characteristics of the human service tool.[2]

The first is the consequence of seeing individuals primarily in terms of their "needs." Each of us can be conceived as a half-glass of water.

We are partly empty. We have deficiencies.

We are also partly full. We have capacities.

Human service professionals focus on deficiencies, call them "needs," and have expert skills in giving each perceived deficiency a label. The negative effects of this diagnostic process have been thoroughly explored in the literature regarding labeling theory.[3] As a result, we are generally aware that to be diagnosed and labeled "mentally ill" or "disadvantaged" carries a heavy negative social consequence.

What is less well understood is the fact that the labeling professions force us, structurally, to focus on the empty half when the appropriate focus may be the full half. For example, many people labeled "developmentally disabled" or "physically disabled" are never going to be "fixed" by the service professions. Nonetheless, they are frequently subjected to years of "training" to write their names or tie their shoes. These same people may have many capacities that are unused and unshared while their lives are surrounded by special services that will demonstrably fail to fix the deficiency. Denying opportunities to express capacities is often the structurally iatrogenic effect of the use of ineffective therapeutic tools.

For those whose "emptiness" cannot be filled by human services, the most obvious "need" is the opportunity to express and share their gifts, skills, capacities, and abilities with friends, neighbors, and fellow citizens in the community. As deficiency-oriented service systems obscure this fact, they inevitably harm their clients *and* the community by preempting the relationship between them.[4]

The second structurally negative effect of the use of the human service tool is its effect on public budgets. It is clear to every elected official that the public purse is limited. Contemporary legislative process is mainly about the division of that purse. To give more to one activity (defense) usually means giving less to another (agriculture or education). Therefore, a realistic approach to public policy and expenditure always requires an understanding of trade-offs—who or what gets less as something else gets more.

This process occurs between major expenditure categories such as education, highways, defense, medicine, and agriculture. Trade-offs also take place within each of these categories. We understand this trade-off, for example, as it is publicly debated about the defense budget. Given a fixed budget, an increase in spending for the Air Force will require a decrease in spending for the Navy. There is a choice to be made.

The same process occurs within the human services budget. Here, however, it is less well understood because the basic competition for the limited funds available for the "disadvantaged" is between the human service system and cash income for labeled people. Service system lobbyists and advocates see the competition for limited public resources as a jockeying between various service providers and systems. They rarely recognize or acknowledge, however, that the net effect of their lobbying is to limit cash income for those they call "needy" and increase the budget and incomes of service programs and providers.

A federal study showed that between 1960 and 1985 federal and state cash assistance programs grew 105 percent in real terms, while noncash programs for services and commodities grew 1,760 percent. By 1985, cash income programs amounted to $32.3 billion, while commodity[5] and service programs received $99.7 billion.[6]

The service system's preemption of public wealth designated for the "disadvantaged" is also demonstrated by studies of poverty allocations in New York City and Chicago.[7] Both studies demonstrate that over 60 percent of all public funds allocated in those cities for low-income people are allocated for services rather than for income.

The effect of trading cash for human services is devastating for people whose lives cannot be "fixed" by service intervention. Nonetheless, we have no effective measures that allow legislators or policymakers to assess whether public investments for services would be more enabling as cash income. As a consequence, most legislative debate surrounding labeled people is about which services to fund, and for how much.

The third structurally negative effect of the human service tool is its impact upon community and associational life. The community, a social space where citizens turn to solve problems, may be displaced by the intervention of human service professionals acting as an alternative method of problem-solving. Human service professionals with special expertise, techniques, and technology push out the problem-solving knowledge and action of friend, neighbor, citizen, and association. As the power of profession and service system ascends, the legitimacy, authority, and capacity of citizens and community descend.[8] The *citizen* retreats. The *client* advances. The power of community action weakens. The authority of the service system strengthens. And as human service tools prevail, the tools of citizenship, association, and community rust. Their uses are even forgotten. Many local people come to believe that the service tool is the only tool, and that their task as good citizens is to support taxes and charities for more services.

The consequence of this professional persuasion is devastating for those labeled people whose primary "need" is to be incorporated in community life and empowered through citizenship. These people include those frequently labeled as developmentally disabled, physically disabled, elderly, or ex-convicts. They desperately "need" incorporation into community life, but the community of citizens and associations has often been persuaded by human service advocates that vulnerable people:

- need to be surrounded by professional services in order to survive;
- are therefore appropriately removed from community life in order to receive these special service programs in special places;
- cannot be incorporated into community life because citizens don't know how to deal with these special people.

The result of this professional pedagogy is a disabled citizenry and impotent community associations, unable to remember or understand how labeled people were or can be included in community life.

Instead of recognizing the crucial need most labeled people have for the empowerment of joining community life as a citizen, expressing capacities and making choices, many good-willed citizens volunteer to assist service systems free of charge. In this simple act, citizen volunteers trade off their unique potential to bring a labeled person into their lives and the associational life of community in exchange for the use of their time as an unpaid agent for a service system. The community group that might ask a disabled or vulnerable person to join as a member decides, instead, to raise money for wheelchairs and rehabilitation centers. The associations of community life are led to support segregated, professionally controlled athletic events rather than incorporating a labeled person into a church bowling league.

In working to meet this need for incorporation, it is necessary to recognize that the human service tool typically limits, weakens, or replaces community, associational, and citizen tools. This is in the nature of any approach built on the premise that vulnerable people will be better because an expert knows better.

The fourth structurally negative consequence of using human service programs is that they can create, in the aggregate, environments that contradict the potential positive effect of any one program. When enough programs surround a client, they may combine to create a new environment in which none of the programs will be effective.

This particular iatrogenic effect is difficult to comprehend because it grows from the simultaneous use of many programs, any one of which might seem reasonable standing alone. Indeed, most individual service programs appear reasonable and "needed" when presented to legislators. What is invisible is the effect of the program when it is joined by many other service programs as they surround a labeled person. With enough services surrounding a life, a new environment emerges that has its own peculiar system of incentives, rewards, and penalties.

The process is analogous to an aggregation of trees. In the urban neighborhood there are usually trees in yards and parkways. We would not say, however, that people in that neighborhood live in a forest, even though the trees in a forest may be of the same kind. We would not call an area a forest until it had enough trees to create a new environment that did not exist in the neighborhood. In the forest, the shade and fallen leaves kill off grasses. In their place appear new wildflowers and bushes. The grassland animals are replaced by those that live in trees. Prairie birds are replaced by forest birds. The forest flora and fauna create a different world; most people even act differently in a forest, even though it is a place comprised of trees familiar to their neighborhood.

By way of analogy, each individual service program is like a tree. But when enough service programs surround people, they come to live in a forest of services. The environment is different from the neighborhood or community. And people who have to live in the service forest will act differently than those people whose lives are principally defined by neighborhood relationships.

We all recognize the forests of services that are called institutions. They are places where people live wholly surrounded by service professionals, programs, and plans. The uniqueness of this environment is emphasized by large buildings, walls, fences, and so on. Nonetheless, a forest of services can be created without walls or large buildings. Places called group homes, halfway houses, and convalescent homes are usually service forests. Also, some labeled individuals who live with their families can be so fully served by professionals that their life is lived in a forest even though their residence is in a neighborhood.

There are also low-income neighborhoods where so many people live lives surrounded by services that the neighborhood itself becomes a forest. People who live in this neighborhood forest are now called the "underclass." This is an obvious misnomer. Instead, we should say that the neighborhood is a place where citizens act as anyone else would if their lives were similarly surrounded and controlled by paid service professionals. A more accurate label than "underclass" would be "dependent on human service systems." A more accurate differentiation of status would be to say the residents are "clients" rather than "citizens."

When the services grow dense enough around people's lives, a circular process develops. A different environment is created for these individuals. The result of a noncommunity environment is that those who experience it necessarily act in unusual and deviant ways. These new ways, called inappropriate behavior, are then cited by service professionals as proof of the need for separation in a forest of services and for more services.

The disabling effect of this circular process is devastating to the client and to our communities. The public is understandably mystified. Each individual program appears to be reasonably needed and appropriate. However, in the aggregate, the programs have become ineffective and often harmful. The situation is analogous to a person who dies of taking twenty different pills, any one of which might have been helpful.

Physicians have long recognized this interactive iatrogenic effect. Service systems have not. Instead, human service systems nearly always prescribe more programs, more services, more "targeting," and large forests. The result is predictably counterproductive. Costs increase. Programs proliferate. Forests grow. Clients multiply. People adapt their behavior to the forest and are called maladaptive. The cycle spirals downward and the failures are blamed on the victims.

In summary, these iatrogenic effects tell us that policymakers and practitioners should be constantly aware that the use of human service tools places a person at risk of a reduced sense of self-worth, poverty, segregation from community life, and disempowerment as a citizen. The risks demand the most serious evaluation of policies that give the power to human service professionals and systems to intervene in the lives of labeled and vulnerable people.

A practical framework for this policy reevaluation would begin by placing the burden of proof upon those who propose a human service intervention as a means of helping a person with a particular condition. This "burden" is analogous to that understood by the Food and Drug Administration as it evaluates the use of various medical interventions. The intervenor has the responsibility to identify the negative side effects and to prove the benefits are greater.

This is an excellent model for evaluating proposed human service interventions. The service advocate should be required to identify the possible negative effects, present evidence of the benefits, and demonstrate that the benefits outweigh the negative effects. The effect of such a rigorous evaluation would create a positive new force in the lives of labeled people. The service agency, department, or professional would be asked by legislators, public executives, boards of directors, foundations, or groups of labeled people to specify the negative effects of their proposals. This wholesome new discipline placed upon the service advocates would create a revolutionary reexamination of their assumptions and practices.

In addition to the burden of proof regarding negative effects and benefits of a *particular* service intervention, the service advocate should also be required to present evidence that the intervention will not be used cumulatively, creating a service forest. Just as the ethical medical professional recognizes and protects against the negative effects of the interaction among many drugs, the human service professional should be required to identify the negative effect of aggregating programs around a person's life and define the safeguards that will be used to protect against the dependency that so frequently result from a "forest" of services.

Once both requirements are met by service advocates and the particular and interactive negative effects are clarified, policymakers should quickly recognize that the use of a particular human service tool is not necessarily good or even neutral. They should see that a service is a potentially injurious tool and begin to ask whether other kinds of nonservice resources, activities, or opportunities might be appropriate for the person said to be in need. They could begin to ask, "Is there a different kind of approach that doesn't involve a human service that might be more effective and have less negative effect?"

Here again, the medical analogy is helpful. While the Food and Drug Administration may approve a medicine as being more beneficial than harmful, an ethical physician does not assume that it should therefore be prescribed. Instead, the physician asks whether there are other, more effective ways of dealing with the condition that do not involve use of the drug and its negative effects.

The current protocol for high blood pressure provides a good example. All the approved medicines have some significant negative effects. Therefore, ethical physicians first seek nonmedical alternatives before risking use of the medicine. This often involves advising clients to undertake an exercise program, reduce their weight, and decrease their salt intake. Similarly, a review of policy options to address conditions of vulnerable and labeled people should systematically examine non–human service responses that might provide the same or better results with fewer or no negative side effects.

This policy options review requires that policymakers have a set of alternatives to test against proposed human service interventions. Fortunately, there are at least three alternatives that have historically proven effective in addressing the conditions of many who are vulnerable, labelable, or said to be in need.

The first option is to identify the capacities, skills, or potential contributions of the persons said to be in need. What policies, resources, or activities could result in the exercise, expression, visibility, and magnification of those assets? For example, many people labeled developmentally disabled have been found to thrive and flourish when they escape a forest of professional services and are provided community opportunities to express their unique gifts.[9] Similarly, low-income people in neighborhoods and public housing developments experience regeneration when they focus on their capacities rather than exclusively upon problems, deficiencies, and needs.[10] However, in the case of both groups of people, the files of the local human service agencies and authorities are filled with descriptions of their needs, deficiencies, diagnoses, and problems. Therefore, those agencies are not useful as a resource for capacity-oriented development. Policymakers will need to find other activities and supports if the assets and capacities of people and communities are to be viewed as the basic problem-solving tools.

The second option is to provide cash income in lieu of access to prepaid or vouchered human services. This option provides an opening to many new opportunities and even creates better services. The advantages of income over services include:

- providing empowering choices in a free market;
- providing choices among services, thus creating a competitive market that should improve services;
- creating a market in low-income areas where mainline enterprises will have an incentive to reach out to low-income people.

There is, of course, the stereotypic concern that "disadvantaged" people might not use their income wisely. However, there is no evidence that, as a group, these people are less wise in the use of their money than doctors, psychologists, social workers, or the other professionals who are now the primary beneficiaries of dollars appropriated for low-income and other labeled people.

The third option is to seek participation in community life and citizenship activities instead of human service interventions. This flows from the fact that many vulnerable people are primarily disabled by their segregation from community life in institutions, "special" programs, or service ghettos.[11] Paradoxically, their lives often improve significantly when they leave service systems and become effectively incorporated in community life.[12] Therefore, the challenge is to create policies that stimulate the hospitality of citizen associations and community groups so that they will incorporate and share the capacities and gifts of those who have been excluded because of their labels.

My purpose in this analysis has been to establish two basic premises:

1. Human service interventions have negative effects as well as benefits.
2. Human service interventions are only one way to address the condition of people who are labeled.

Many of our failed reforms and programs during the years since World War II are the result of our failure to recognize these two realities. When policymakers begin to evaluate human service proposals from the perspective of these two premises, we will create much more effective means of problem-solving. Making these premises operational is reasonably simple. They can be expressed in five basic questions that can be asked by any person responsible for policies affecting those citizens who are especially vulnerable, disadvantaged, or exploited:

1. What are the negative effects of the human service proposed to help the class of people?
2. What are the situations in which the proposed service may be applied with many other services and what interactive negative effects will result?
3. Will a focus on the capacities of the class of people be more effective than a service program's focus on deficiencies and needs?
4. Will providing the dollars proposed for funding the human service provide greater benefits if given to the clients as cash income?
5. Will incorporation into community life be more beneficial than special, separating service treatments?

The last three questions incorporate the central values of a free and democratic society. They recognize that the greatest "service" our society provides is the opportunity to express our unique capacities, to have a decent income, and to join with our fellow citizens in creating productive communities. No human service professional or program will ever equal the healing and empowering effect of those three democratic opportunities. Therefore, policies that support citizen capacity, income, and community should have preference over other forms of intervention that are necessarily second-rate and second-best responses.

Redefining Community

It was in a small New England town that I first understood the limits of community services. The town was located in a state with one of the most humane and progressive systems for serving people who are labeled developmentally disabled. Very few were in large institutions, small group homes had proliferated, sheltered workshops were being dismantled, and a serious effort was under way in the schools to bring labeled children into the regular classrooms. In this town, I was taken to one of the group homes. The home was physically indistinguishable from the other houses on the street. Living in the house were five middle-aged men, most of whom had lived there for nearly ten years.

It was with considerable pride that an agency director and a public official took me to visit these men. They wanted me to see how their clients were "a part of the community" and the beneficiaries of an effective program of community services. When the opportunity came to talk to each of the men, I inquired about their lives, experiences, and relationships in the town. To my surprise, the response of each man made clear that they had almost no social relationships with their neighbors or the other citizens of the town. None of them could identify a close local friend or neighbor, and none were involved in any kind of organization, association, or club. When I asked the staff members whether they knew of any social relationships the men had in the community, they were unable to identify any other than a few shopkeepers.

Later I learned, by talking with other people within the state human service system, that the isolated circumstances of these five men tended to be the rule rather than the exception. Nonetheless, they were described as "deinstitutionalized," as being "in the community," and as receiving "community services." That was when I first realized that all of this community language obscured the basic fact that these men were completely isolated from community while surrounded by community services.

One wonders how it is possible, in a small town of 5,000 people, to find a typical house and have five residents live there for ten years without any effective community relationships. Yet human service systems designed to provide what are called "community services" often have managed to do just that.

Perhaps the issue can be clarified by defining "community services" more accurately. I would not want to suggest that these are services that will "make people part of community." Rather, I mean to point out that services provided in small towns or neighborhoods should not be called community services if they do not involve people in community relationships. Indeed, what are now called community services are often the major barriers to involvement in the community. Let's say, then, that the system in this state is now providing *local services*, not community services. And that the relocation of those services to local places has had almost no positive effect on the participation of labeled people in community life.

This failure of integration clearly limits the lives of the labeled people themselves. But the exclusion also limits the experience of local citizens. Most community members have infrequent opportunities to be joined in their common life by people who have been given one of the labels established by the service industry. Indeed, the common life of North America is so segregated that the absence of experience with those who are excluded has led many citizens to imagine that labeled people are somehow inappropriate for community life. Many have come to believe that labeled people are so incapacitated that their lives literally depend upon separate and expert attention. Having accepted this proposition, most citizens lead lives in which they can only imagine, never see or talk to, labeled people.

What Is Community?

How can incorporation of labeled people into community life be achieved? Before we can respond to that question, we must ask: What do we mean by community?

There is no universally accepted definition. However, one is so practically useful that it can become central to the work of those concerned about the incorporation of labeled people into community life.

I am referring to an understanding laid out by Alexis de Tocqueville, the French count who visited the United States in 1831. What he found was that European settlers were creating a society different from the one they knew in Europe: communities formed around an uncustomary social invention, small groups of common citizens coming together to form organizations that solve problems.

Tocqueville observed three features in how these groups operated. First, they were groups of citizens who decided they had the power to decide what was a problem. Second, they decided they had the power to decide how to solve the problem. Third, they often decided that they would themselves become the key actors in implementing the solution. From Tocqueville's perspective, these citizen associations were a uniquely powerful instrument being created in America, the foundation stones of American communities.

It should seem obvious that communities are collective associations. They are more than and different from a series of friendships. One can have a friendship with a labeled person in an institution, for example, but that does not mean the person has been incorporated into the community. A community is more than just a place. It comprises various groups of people who work together on a face-to-face basis in public life, not just in private.

The kinds of associations that express and create community take several forms. Many of them are relatively formal, with names and with officers elected by the members. They may be the American Legion, the church bowling league, or the local peace fellowship.

A second kind of association is not so formal. It usually has no officers or name. Nonetheless, it represents a gathering of citizens who solve problems, celebrate together, or enjoy their social compact. These associations could be a poker club, a coffee klatch, or a gathering of neighbors who live on the block. The fact that they do not have a formal name and structure should not obscure the fact that they are often the sites of critical dialogue, opinion formation, and decision-making that influence the values and problem-solving capacities of citizens. Indeed, many Americans are primarily influenced in their decision-making and value formation by these informal groups.

A third form of association is less obvious because one could describe the place where it occurs as an enterprise or business. However, much associational activity takes place in restaurants, beauty parlors, barbershops, bars, hardware stores, and other places of business. People gather in these places for interaction as well as transaction. In the eighteenth century, some of the most basic discussions about the formation of the government of the United States and its Constitution occurred in inns and taverns, and similar settings provide the backdrop for some of the most fundamental associational life today.

These three types of associations represent the community from which most labeled people are excluded, and into which they need to be incorporated if they are to become active citizens at the associational center of a democratic society.[1]

Including the Excluded

Once we have understood the nature of the community of associations, we can begin to look at ways to incorporate excluded people into this community life. Some people who have been excluded forge a path back into community on their own. This is usually a heroic struggle that requires great commitment and persistence. And while we know that this escape into inclusion is infrequent, it is equally clear that life in the community is the dream of many of those labeled people whose lives are surrounded by nothing but services.[2]

A second point of entry into community life is created by family and friends, who almost always have a vision for the labeled individual that reaches beyond access to community services. They see that the good life is not just a fully serviced life, but a life filled with the care, power, and continuity that come from being part of a community.

A third point of entry into community is the one I would like to focus on in this article. It is a process involving individuals who assume a special responsibility for guiding excluded people out of service and into the realm of the community. In varying degrees, this phenomenon occurs in many places.

Northwestern University's Center for Urban Affairs and Policy Research has engaged in a continuing study of the initiatives of these individuals who serve as "community guides." The guides are unique, unschooled in their efforts, and informed by their own individual creativity and insight. While it is difficult to generalize about these people, it is possible to describe some patterns of their work.

Building Community Relationships

Effective guides do not just introduce one person to another: They bring a person into the web of associational life that can act as a powerful force in that person's life. And they bring the individual into life as a citizen by incorporating him into relationships where his capacities can be expressed—where he is not simply defined by his "deficiencies."

Most guides are people with a special eye for the gift, the potential, the interest, the skills, the smile, the capacity of those who are said to be "in special need." Focusing upon these strengths, they introduce people into community life. Several guides we interviewed had previously worked in service systems, and told us they had not realized that their entire understanding of the people they called clients was focused upon "fixing" them. They report that their most basic change in attitude, allowing them to be a guide, was to stop trying to "fix" people.

A second attribute of most, but not all, effective guides is that they are well-connected in the interrelationships of community life. They have invested much of life's energy and vitality in associational activity. Because of these connections, they are able to make a variety of contacts quickly because "they know people who know other people." This is why most guides come from community life rather than service systems. A person interested in human services can spend money and receive training that will give the capacity to fix others. There is, however, no school, program, curriculum, or money that can connect a person to associational community life. Instead, this capacity grows stronger from years of experience and contribution to community life.

The third common characteristic of community guides is that they achieve their ends because they are trusted by their community peers, and not because they have institutional authority. This point is a correlate of the second. If guides are well connected, it is because they are trusted, and that trust is the result of their having invested their lives and commitments in the lives of others in the informal web of associational life.

In working through a framework of trust, the guides do not identify themselves with systems. They do not say that they are from the Department of Mental Deficiency, Division of Experimentation, Bureau of Community Programs. Instead, they say, "I'm a friend of your sister Mary, and she said that I should ask you about the choir that you direct. I have a friend who loves to sing and has a beautiful voice, and I think that you might like to have her in your choir." In this way, the guide is introducing an excluded person based on her capacity to sing. She is making the introduction through a relationship with a trusted relative. She is seeking engagement of the excluded person in an association of community life—a local choir. In two sentences, the guide is able to bring together the capacity, the connectedness, and the trust that are the visible pathways into community life.

The fourth characteristic of almost all community guides is that they believe strongly that the community is a reservoir of hospitality that is waiting to be offered. It is their job to lead someone to ask for it.

This belief in a hospitable community is a critical ingredient in the work of successful guides. Their vivacious expectations of success make it clear that they are "making an offer you can't refuse" when they introduce an excluded person to a citizen active in associational life. They are not apologetic or begging or asking for charity or help. Instead, they are enthusiastically presenting the gift of an excluded person to the hospitality of a person active in the community.

In our experience, we have found that guides' belief in a hospitable community is well founded. Indeed, many guides find that their belief in the community grows even greater as they consistently find that there is a broad community readiness to incorporate people who have been excluded. This is not to say that every person in every neighborhood is hospitable—we all know this is not the case. But the guides we interviewed report that the great majority of people they have encountered are receptive and open to diversity. It is the obvious task of the guide to relate to this part of the community rather than to focus on those who are negative or resistant.

Unfortunately, many people in human service systems have

had negative experiences as they have tried to parachute small institutions called group homes into neighborhoods. Frequently, the local residents will resist this professional vision of "community integration." However, the very same neighbors, asked to meet and involve one person named Sam Jones who has been labeled developmentally disabled, will frequently welcome that person into their collective life. Just as every individual has capacities and deficiencies, every community has hospitality and rejection. A community guide knows the terrain of hospitality and avoids the pitfall of rejection.

A fifth characteristic of most effective community guides is that they learn that they must say goodbye to the person they guide into community life. This is not a natural step. Nonetheless, most guides report that they have learned that in order for the fullness of community hospitality to be expressed and the excluded person to be wholly incorporated as a citizen, they must leave the scene. They are guides, not servants.[3]

Policy Paths to Inclusion

While most guides are people who do not need "policies" to guide them and are, in fact, unsure of what a policy is, there are those in human service systems who need policies in order to understand practice. For such policy and system operatives, it is possible to summarize the work of guides in the following policy statement: "It is our policy to reduce dependence on human services by increasing interdependence in community life through a focus on the gifts and capacities of people who have been excluded from community life because of their labels."

Contained in this policy statement is the recognition that there are many dependency-creating human services. It is those services that the guides attempt to replace with associational life. However, it is also clear that there are human services that do not create dependence and could be designed to support community life, such as income supplements, independent living aides, and specialized medical services. There has been very little systematic study in this area. A preliminary hypothesis is that services that are heavily focused on deficiency tend to be pathways out of community and into the exclusion of serviced life. We need a rigorous examination of public investments so that we can distinguish between services that lead people out of community and into dependency and those activities that support people in community life.[4]

Finally, we are reminded that the policy statement indicates that it is our goal to "increase interdependence in community life." It is critical here that we emphasize the word *interdependence*. The goal is not to create independence—except from social service systems. Rather, we are recognizing that every life in community is, by definition, interdependent—filled with trusting relationships and empowered by the collective wisdom of citizens in discourse.

Community is about the common life that is lived in such a way that the unique creativity of each person is a contribution to the other. The crisis we have created in the lives of excluded people is that they are disassociated from their fellow citizens. We cannot undo that terrible exclusion by a thoughtless attempt to create illusory independence. Nor can we undo it by creating a friendship with a person who lives in exclusion.

Our goal should be clear. We are seeking nothing less than a life surrounded by the richness and diversity of community. A collective life. A common life. An everyday life. A powerful life that gains its joy from the creativity and connectedness that come when we join in association to create an inclusive world.

A Reconsideration of the Crisis
of the Welfare State

There is a rapidly growing concern by both the left and right regarding the apparently limitless demands upon public budgets of social welfare programs. The competing demands for reindustrialization, tax limitations, or armaments are accentuating this widely reported "crisis of the welfare state." The typical response has been a policy debate that focuses upon issues such as setting "ceilings," establishing new priorities, cutting back selective programs, and eliminating ineffective programs.

These policies generally attempt to control four areas of public expenditure: medical services; programmatic social services such as child care, counseling, training, and drug abuse therapy; pension programs providing income for those of older age; and income or income subsidies for those of "employable" age.

A policy discussion involving the limitations of these four elements of the welfare sector is useful because it demonstrates the effective boundaries of this definition of the problem. Each element of the welfare sector presents special, resilient characteristics that have successfully resisted limiting strategies.

Medical services relentlessly increase their fiscal demand while their impact upon health status steadily declines. Indeed, medical expenditures and improved health status now appear to have very little relationship. Therefore, the most common policy response has been an attempt to place arbitrary limits on medical costs or services as a rationing mechanism. This policy is countered by reports of radical new medical breakthroughs with high-cost technologies.

Programmatic social services have rapidly increased their jurisdiction over a variety of social relationships and the percentage of the population receiving each variety. Because these services are highly labor-intensive and the level of skill required is so low, their expansion has created a large labor force of service workers. These workers are largely drawn from the middle and working classes and women initially entering the labor force. As a group, these workers represent a potent popular force whose limited income is critical to their survival. The necessity for their service grows less obvious, however, as they expand into new fields such as grief counseling and institutionally paid patient advocacy. These newly invented marginal categories of need primarily serve to create jobs for those of middle age by imputing new maladies to those of young and old age. While the programmatic services have not found the equivalent of a medical breakthrough to fuel new demand, the breadth of the space they occupy in the marketplace and the political power of their associations are an effective countermeasure to policies of limitation.

Pension programs are impelled by three relentless forces. First, the demographics of most industrialized societies show a rapidly increasing percentage of older people. Second, the shrinking demand for labor in technological societies demands new allocations of the growing supply of nonemployment. Third, in order to grow, the medical and social service sectors need enlarged populations to serve. The older person as a dependent client is essential to the rationalization of the growing service sector. Policymakers with the intent to limit pension expenditures experience the potent political counterforce of the pensioners, the service workers, and the children of older parents.

Income or income subsidy programs are reflected in at least three variations: direct cash support; income in exchange for public-sector work, called "workfare" in the United States; and income subsidy for work in the private sector. These forms of income support have been most vulnerable to limitation and cutting back because the recipients involved are the least powerful. Those who are beneficiaries are limited in number and generally the least powerful in society. The fact that they receive a cash subsidy may also mean that they receive only limited political support from medical and service workers, who prefer the clients insured by medical and social service programs. Nonetheless, it is clear that public and private policymakers are now developing long-range plans based on the assumption that a substantial percentage of the population will be continuously unemployed or receiving subsidized employment. Normalizing structural unemployment appears to be the new order, institutionalizing the underclass and depending on public conscience to provide the motive for maintenance at marginal levels.

This review of the social welfare sector and its constituencies demonstrates the problems faced by those who seek policies supporting limits, ceilings, or cutbacks. The reality is that an approach focused upon limiting or reducing public budgets finds a powerful counterforce composed of medical professionals and their allied service and product industries, popular supporters of medical expansion who hope for immortality through medical miracles, social workers of all classes together with their ever-growing dependent populations, women seeking a new place in the labor market, older people and their children, the unemployed, and those who believe in decent levels of support for the disadvantaged. The powerful nature of these interests, each deeply invested in serving and being served, makes it quite clear that a *significant* change in the costs of the social welfare sector is unlikely to occur through the forces of fiscal reform.

Indeed, the reality is that the social welfare system is not really a sector. It is better understood as the natural child of modern techniques and technology, professional dominance, authority of central systems over social relations, and universalizing expectations for participation in the paid workforce.

These four parents, committed to the growth and development of their systems, will necessarily nurture and, perhaps inadvertently, strengthen the child's power of self-defense. Indeed, the question of reforming social welfare is essentially a family problem, unlikely to be resolved until the parents are prepared to change themselves.

Approached as a special economic problem, we believe that significant change in the social welfare system is illusory. The system serves broad interests and performs critical functions in our technological societies. Therefore, if we pursue technological imperatives, it is unreasonable to think we will abandon so useful a child.

The reasonable question is to ask whether the conditions the social welfare system purports to deal with might be starting points for parental reform. Could we identify, or imagine, some beginnings that address social dilemmas in such a way that the excesses of technology, professionalization, centralism, and commodification might be bounded or even challenged? An inquiry of this nature could lead us toward defining possibilities worthy of our purpose and pursuit.

Such an inquiry begins with the premise so well defined by Paul Goodman when he said, "The good society cannot be the substitution of a new order for an old order. Rather, it is the extension of spheres of free action until they make up most of social life." Social welfare systems are the new order of a technological society.

We propose here to suggest a framework to examine the nature of spheres for free action, the possibility of their extension, and the policies that might allow their proliferation. Their focus is primarily, but not exclusively, those conditions that are the object of social welfare.

A Different Sphere of Action

We would suggest that spheres for free action incorporate these interdependent characteristics: opportunities for choices, authoritative local forums, and appropriate tools. Social welfare systems are the progeny of systems that invert these characteristics by producing social monopolies through centralized decision-making. To begin an inquiry into the possibilities of extending spheres of free action, a series of questions is suggested.

Choice

The reality of life defined by social welfare systems is that it creates a monopoly on forms of action and legitimate actors. To extend spheres of free action, these monopolies must be bent, broken, avoided, or ignored. Questions:

1. Where have communities and individuals maintained effective choices?
2. Where have communities and individuals pushed back monopolies on actions and actors?
3. What are the monopolistic features of choices within the welfare system?

   a. Are people required to take professional service in lieu of income?
   b. Are people required to use professionals to deal with their conditions?
   c. Are people required to accept professional definitions of their problem?
   d. What are the incentives and penalties for not accepting the system's definition of your problem, the appropriate intervenor, and the form of intervention?

4. What form of public action could push back these monopolies and broaden spheres for free action? Are there policies and constituencies with the interest and capacity to take such action?
5. Are there public actions that could encourage inventions and initiatives that operate outside the boundaries of the monopolies? Would these actions merely

create new rules and/or provide a vehicle for "plugging" informal efforts into the system?

It should be noted that there are those who urge demonopolization and favor competitive or marketplace models. This approach creates intensive commodification and, if current experience in the United States is a prospective model, will produce remonopolization in the private corporate sector. Therefore, to extend spheres of free action must mean the democratization of both definition and action at the local level.

Forum

Much of the social welfare system is compensation for the technological society's destruction of social life and its tools. This atomization has degraded or eliminated the forums where community definition and action can be conceived or negotiated. Thus, care is translated from an expression of community to a commodity of professions or marketeers. The possibility of extending spheres of free action requires the restoration of the forum—places where polities, face to face, can invent, negotiate, and decide upon choices with authority. This is actually another form of demonopolization of central state and/or corporate authority as well as the monotonic electronic substitute for the dialogue of citizens. Questions:

1. Where have communities maintained effective forums for invention and decision-making? (This does not include those advisory groups or other forms of community support engineered by social welfare managers.)
2. Where have communities extended their authority to define and decide? What made these openings possible?
3. Are there legitimate limits that should be placed upon the authority of local communities to act on conditions involving care and well-being?
4. What are the major interests that would oppose this relocation of authority?

5. What forms of public action would create incentives in support of authoritative local forums?

It should be noted that some bureaucratic decentralists have conceived and initiated franchiselike local community expressions. They have the apparent power to make decisions, but the control of basic budgets and tools for carrying out decisions is maintained and defined by the central authority. Effectively, this translates into the statement that, "At the locality, you can decide upon anything I agree to pay for or that can be achieved with my tools."

Tools

The social welfare system is itself the tool of a technological society for producing service in lieu of care, and commodification in lieu of well-being. Its basic technology is its system, an adaptation of the bureaucratic/corporate model. This model has sometimes been cloned at the local level as a substitute for expanding spheres of free action.

To expand the choice-making capacities of authoritative forums, it is necessary to push back the method (technologies) of the social welfare system as well as its control over budgets and other tools. This means the *transfer* of appropriate material and economic resources from one sphere to the other. Free action finally depends upon the power of definition, creation, access, and control over appropriate tools. Questions:

1. Where have communities and individuals maintained effective control over the economics and technology for care and well-being?
2. Where have communities recently extended their control over these economies and technologies? What made these openings possible?
3. What new local inventions have created appropriate tools or action-expanding economics for local production for local use?
4. What use-oriented activities have been maintained,

created, or extended in localities? What made these openings possible?

5. How has information about new tools and economies been shared with others?
6. What public actions could extend the access to productive local tools and economies? What interests would oppose this extension? Which polities would support the extension?

Public Policy Addendum

In thinking about extending spheres of free action, one is constantly impressed by the barriers imposed by various forms of state regulation. These barriers are portrayed as public protections, but they are usually means to ensure professional monopolies, central authority, and preferred technologies. Therefore, one can see that one form of state action allied to extending spheres is removing barriers to free action. Practically speaking, this means placing limits upon monopolies over social choice, forum, and tools. Questions:

1. Which public barriers disadvantage community choices, forums, and tools?
2. What would be the costs to general well-being of their removal?
3. Which polities would support their removal?

The idea of deregulation invites state action to remove its own barriers to *extending spheres.* There is in this idea the assumption that the essential problem is barriers to extension. In some societies it may be more accurate, however, to describe the motion and direction of the problem in different terms. In these societies the problem is best understood as the rapid *invasion of spheres* of free action by technologically based systems. Rather than policies allowing extension, the basic problem is better understood as defending existing spheres from invasion.

This raises the question as to whether it is possible to provide a policy framework for two domains—technological systems and spheres of free action. Can we create structures that will foster dualism by removing barriers to the spheres, or is the reality that the technical systems will necessarily drive out the spheres of free action unless there are positive actions to protect the spheres from invasion?

Perhaps a metaphorical example will make the point. In the United States, many rural communities were composed of family farms. As chemical-based, high-tech, machine-oriented farming was introduced by agricultural professionals from universities, those farmers who did not adapt to the technological system found their farms to be uneconomical, and they sold out.

The remaining family farmers inundated their land with chemicals and pesticides, borrowed heavily to buy expensive machinery, managed their operation with home computers, and are now finding that no amount of technology can make their farms economical. They are now being squeezed out of farming by agribusinesses. Therefore, in many rural states, legislators are belatedly considering legislation that will "protect the family farm." This "protectionist" legislation recognizes that no amount of family, local, or community compliance with the demands of techno-agriculture will allow for survival. Therefore, the legislation attempts to designate an economic and social space protected from the demands of the technological system.

Are we in essentially the same situation in regard to that social space encompassing spheres of free action? If so, is state protection for free space desirable or possible? If it is both, what is the nature of the state protections necessary to allow survival of free space in a technological society?

The Criminal
Justice System

Thinking About Crime, Sacrifice, and Community

It was many years ago that I had my first contact with the correctional field. A warden of a county jail serving a large city suggested that I tour his institution. The gentleman was well prepared for his responsibilities, for he had both a law degree and a doctorate in sociology with special emphasis upon deviance.

When we had completed the tour, we stood on a catwalk overlooking a vast room. It was filled with picnic tables. Suspended from the catwalk at each corner of the room was a television set. Seated at the picnic tables were more than a thousand men. Some watched the television, some talked, some played cards, many stared. Almost all of them were young. Almost all were black.

As we looked down upon this scene, I asked my correctional colleague how much time the men spent in the room. He told me that except for meals, one hour in a small yard outdoors, and cell time, they spent all their time in this room.

Because he could see that I was troubled by this form of treatment, he told me something that summarized all of his scholarship and experience. "You may not realize this," he said, "but you are observing the only method of rehabilitation that we are sure works. These men are aging. When they reach a certain time in their late twenties or early thirties, they will stop engaging in the behavior that brought them here. You see," he assured me, "the one thing we know for sure is that as people grow older their tendency to engage in most types of violent crimes rapidly declines."

We both stood silently and looked over the hundreds of men seated at the picnic tables. And I saw them for the first time through the eyes of a correctional official. I saw them there, all aging. As each second ticked away, normality grew closer. It was an apparently satisfying vision for my correctional colleague. It gave his work meaning in a situation that otherwise might have been a scene of surrealistic meaninglessness.

Since that day I have never had the opportunity to talk to another professional in corrections. Therefore, I am unaware of whether the state of correctional science has changed from the understanding of my learned friend.

I am aware, however, that there are scholars today whose conclusions are much the same as those of my correctional colleague. It is my further understanding that these scholars are also persuaded that even the aging process fails for a significant number of people. In this predicted failure, they also see the appropriateness of execution.

For those who hold this viewpoint, it is a curiously satisfying, indeed benign, understanding of crime, criminality, and corrections. Deviance appears, afflicts, is healed by time— except on those unfortunate occasions when its cure is necessarily death-imposed.

As an understanding, it does, however, seem absent of the benefits of human intervention beyond the sporadic work of the executioner. Indeed, one wonders why an expert in corrections is needed at all in this world ruled by the march of time.

With great respect for those learned scholars and associated consultants whose science finds in behalf of the aging process, it is nonetheless reasonable to inquire into the possibilities of other means to rehabilitate.

It is a curious notion, this modern idea of rehabilitation. One hears it said that "He is being rehabilitated," much as one hears that an ill person is being cured. This therapeutic understanding is confirmed by the fact that there are all kinds of inventions called "treatment modalities." Indeed, a careful reading of the rehabilitation literature confirms that it is not the therapeutic ideology but the ideology of *allopathic* therapy that appears to guide the rehabilitative professions. This is quite natural, of course, because those of us residing in the United States have a deep faith in the understanding of allopathic medicine—the healing philosophy that guides those professionals with the letters M.D. after their names. Nonetheless, it is also true that this allopathic understanding is only one of tens of thousands of healing methods that are being and have been practiced by humankind in the pursuit of healing and regeneration.

What is most significant about the allopathic approach is the radical nature of its basic premise. For along the continuum of world healing practices, allopathic medicine stands at one pole—an extremist premise. Its radical position grows from the unique belief that the malady is *in* the person and the cure is achieved by professional intrusion *into* that person. In that understanding the allopathic faith stands isolated in therapeutic history as it ignores both the world around the person and the person as healers. Instead, it emphasizes the malady within and the expert assault upon that pathogen.

In contrast, nearly all other regenerative ideas comprehend an inextricable relationship between the person and the social and physical world in which he or she resides, and an immutable force in the person's own will to heal. So it is that most time-tested healing rites convene community, draw power from the earth, and call on the spirit of the afflicted.

Allopathic therapy and its ideology, on the other hand, disperse community, isolate the afflicted, and call on the spirit of expert intervention. It is an exceptional belief. And it is upon the foundations of this extremist understanding that our rehabilitative sciences are built today.

Whether or not one believes that the allopathic belief system is the true faith of healing, it certainly does not follow that its unique physiologically based premises are appropriate to analysis or action relating to crime, criminality, and corrections. Indeed, it is more reasonable to suggest that this radical theory, designed to address the treatment of duodenal ulcers, is not likely to provide either effective theory or practice regarding those who seem not to respect the property or persons of others.

The rehabilitative sciences appear then to be allopathic captives. And yet we know that allopathic medicine was not even a significant factor in the great health advances that have doubled our life expectancy in the last two centuries. As the great English epidemiologist Thomas McKeown has so elegantly demonstrated, the great improvements in our health were caused by action by communities to change the environment. Our great leap forward in health was caused by our collective decisions to purify water, separate waste, and pasteurize milk. Allopathic medicine was practically a bystander.

Therefore, if we choose to follow an analogous ideology in pursuit of rehabilitation, the *health model* rather than the medical model should guide us. Indeed, the medical model is increasingly understood as a counterproductive faith that fails to recognize the wholeness of people, their land, and their community. This counterproductivity is so widespread that studies of the iatrogenic effects (doctor-created disease) led the Centers for Disease Control to predict that during 1986 there would be more than 80,000 deaths due to hospital treatment by allopathic medicine. It is no wonder, then, that those rehabilitation efforts modeled after allopathic medicine should be found wanting, for allopathic medicine has not been a major contributor to our health and is now scientifically recognized as a significant cause of the very maladies it seeks to cure.

For this reason, it strikes me that the rehabilitation field will begin to achieve a respected place in society when it breaks free of its allopathic captivity. At the center of this liberation will be the recognition that treatment doesn't work. Communities work. And working communities both prevent crime and heal criminals. Thus, the *possible* future will reach beyond allopathy, therapy, and even deinstitutionalization to what might be called recommunalization—a recognition that it is in person, place, and peers that possibilities of regenerative community occur.

In this understanding, I can commend to you the work of Dr. Jerome Miller of the National Center on Institutions and Alternatives. They have pioneered the reconstruction of community *and* the convicted in a national program that calls upon local associations and organizations to build themselves by helping in the regeneration of others.

It should be noted, incidentally, that this program in reincorporation (to make a whole body) is paralleled by exciting new efforts by other groups that seek to do the same thing with people labeled mentally ill, developmentally disabled, physically disabled, and elderly. It is in alliance with these pioneer efforts at recommunalization that the corrections field can escape its counterproductive fascination with treatment and become a participant in the rehabilitation of community life that can both prevent criminality and rehabilitate the offenders.

The best description of this developing movement in the United States is Robert Woodson's book *A Summons to Life*. In his national search for working examples of prevention and rehabilitation, he found that the prevention of crime, the rehabilitation of persons, and the reconstruction of community are not three ideas. They are one idea, spoken in three different ways. I commend Woodson's book because it gives cases and guidelines toward a recommunalizing path for rehabilitation.

There is, then, great hope ahead for a wholistic, community-building rehabilitation movement. At the same time, I fear there is one great barrier to this hope. To recognize the barrier, we need to return to the catwalk of the county jail where the warden saw a thousand men aging toward rehabilitation.

Among the thousand men, over 900 were black. In the

county serviced by the jail, less than 20 percent of the people are black.

How do we explain this disproportion, for it is a disproportion of extreme selectivity? It strikes me that there are two traditional explanations for the disproportion. The first is that the persons incarcerated are genetically deficient. This racist view, whether held by bigots, geneticists, or new-breed social scientists, is unworthy of our civilized consideration.

The second explanation has it that these young black men are the result of a disproportionate experience with a poor environment created by a history of slavery, racism, and poverty that now expresses itself in joblessness, poor schools, terrible housing, and so forth. And all of this is true, absolutely and devastatingly true. But it doesn't really explain the *radical* nature of the disproportion, for a significant proportion of the nonblack population also faces joblessness, poor schools, and terrible housing. But they do not appear at the jail picnic tables in anything like appropriate numbers.

In the years since I stood on that catwalk, the reality of the radical disproportion has continued to persist. And the reason for the overwhelming incarceration and execution of young black men has continued to test my understanding.

Therefore, we may need to search for the answer in disciplines other than sociology or psychology. My own sense is that the 900 black men at the picnic tables are more likely explained by anthropology or history. Let me suggest an understanding drawn from those disciplines.

We know, historically, that across hemispheres and through time, most societies have engaged in sacrificial offerings. Animals have been sacrificed and people have been sacrificed. The Mayans chose to sacrifice young virgins. The Puritans chose to sacrifice women they believed to be witches. The Germans chose to sacrifice Jews.

This will to sacrifice is found across cultures and throughout time. Its persistence is remarkable. And its roots are deep within Western society, rooted in the Judeo-Christian tradition. The practice is clearly described by Paul, speaking to the

Hebrews about Moses. He says that Moses "took the blood of calves and of goats, with water and scarlet wool, and sprinkled both the book and all the people. . . . Moreover, he sprinkled with blood both the tabernacle and all the vessels of the ministry. And almost all things are by the law purged with blood. And without shedding of blood there is no redemption." So we know that our culture, like most others, has been deeply committed to the idea that in sacrificial acts, guilt is overcome and regeneration is possible.

While the sacrificial concept is nearly universal, those who are to be sacrificed are unpredictable. Virgins in the Yucatán, grandmothers in Salem, Jews in Buchenwald—each is the peculiar sacrifice of a people in search of renewal and freedom from guilt.

It is impolite these days to suggest that we may be a people with a history and culture linked to all humankind. Nonetheless, it might also be foolish to suggest that we are a people unique and free of the will to sacrifice. Indeed, it is possible that we are actually the children of our Mayan, Puritan, and German ancestors. And that the radical disproportion of young black men is basically explained as our form of sacrifice. We may hide it behind gray walls, rather than sprinkling blood in the public tabernacle. We may execute in the darkest hours of the night, rather than at high noon on a pyramid. But that may be because we are ashamed that we are still engaged in human sacrifice.

If we are so engaged, then there is a terrible truth we must face. And it is this:

The Mayans sacrificed virgins because they mistakenly believed that these young women were the purest and best offering they could make to the gods.

The Germans sacrificed the Jews because they mistakenly believed that the Jews were representatives of evil and that purity depended upon a purge. The Puritans sacrificed women they called witches for the same reason.

But we are different. We do not believe, I suspect, that young black men are symbols of purity or that they represent demonic forces. Even the new academic conservatives would admit that the young black men are a sociological phenomenon, expressions of terrible environments. But we still deprive them of liberty and life as did the Mayans, the Puritans, and the Germans. But unlike them, we *know* that the young black men are creations of a world *we* made, rather than a world of devils, witches, virgins, and gods.

If we choose, then, to sacrifice those whose world we created, it should indeed be done behind high walls and in the deep of night. For we haven't even the integrity of those whose mistaken beliefs were that the sacrificed were the embodiments of purity or devilry.

It would indeed be a degraded civilization that consistently inflicted its worst upon those it *knew* to be the result of a history of subjugation. It could never relieve its guilt by sacrificing those who were creations of that history. The history would live on no matter the number of young black men whose lives were sacrificed.

We cannot kill our history. We cannot sacrifice enough people to hide the truth that the evil in our time is what the eminent African-American social psychologist Ken Clark has called the "dark ghetto," and not the people who live within it.

William James noted our apparent human fondness for war. Therefore, he suggested that we would not end war until we found a moral equivalent for war. It may also be the case that we will not end human sacrifice until we find its moral equivalent. I suspect that our penal institutions consistently fail to rehabilitate because they are largely places of human sacrifice. They may not change until we end their sacrificial function. Therefore, the possibility of correctional reform may require the moral equivalent of sacrifice.

Let me propose, then, that we sacrifice the ghetto. That we take our sacrificial nature and use it to offer up to God a Heavenly City—Dr. King's city, where rich men and poor men, black children and white children, may live in justice, free of human sacrifice forever.

These reflections were informed by the lives of two people. The first is Judith Snow, a woman whose life has been lived without the power to move any of her body. She taught me about the use of human sacrifice, and reminded me that I should ask those who are to be sacrificed to speak for themselves. She told me that at least one such voice ought to be heard in this chapter.

Therefore, I conclude with some of the words of Daniel Morris Thomas, as recorded by the Associated Press on April 15, 1986:

> Kicking, cursing, and fighting with five prison guards, Daniel Morris Thomas was strapped into Florida's electric chair today and executed for shooting a man and raping his wife as her husband lay dying.
>
> A prison spokesman said the struggle was the first to take place in Florida State Prison's execution chamber within memory.
>
> Cursing and screaming, "Get off me!" the 37-year-old inmate was subdued after a seven-minute struggle.
>
> "It was violent," said Vernon Bradford, a prison spokesman, referring to Mr. Thomas' struggle in the death chamber. "It was the first time this has happened in my experience."
>
> Mr. Thomas, a member of the ski-mask gang that rampaged through rural central Florida for 10 months in 1975 and 1976, was convicted of murdering Charles Anderson, 48, a professor at the University of Florida, on New Year's Day 1976. The killer raped Mrs. Anderson as her husband bled to death in their home in rural Polk County.
>
> Officials said the gang was responsible for two murders, five rapes, and several beatings in a 10-month rampage. The police said the crimes were racially motivated; all the victims were white.
>
> After he was seated in the electric chair Mr. Thomas,

who was about six feet tall and weighed 180 pounds, slid down into the chair, his legs thrashing at the men trying to restrain him.

The guards finally managed to pin Mr. Thomas to the chair, and a strap was placed around his chin.

The prison superintendent, Richard Dugger, then approached the condemned man, leaned over and spoke to him, apparently telling him he would not be able to read his last statement unless he stopped struggling.

Mr. Thomas then quieted and began reading from a yellow legal sheet in a low voice to the 19 witnesses who had watched the struggle through large windows.

"We are human tools, political pawns, political human sacrifices for the politicians," Mr. Thomas said, referring to Florida's 241 prisoners on death row.

The switch was thrown at 12:14 P.M., and the inmate was pronounced dead five minutes later.

Rethinking Our National Incarceration Policy

The most significant function of the criminal justice system is to compensate for the limits and failures of society's other major systems. That compensation could result in deterrence, removal, or reformation. However, none of these results reforms the other system failures. Indeed, incarceration may actually deter reform by removing from sight and mind those who are the products or victims of failed economic, political, or social systems.

From this perspective, the fact that the United States now incarcerates more people per capita than any other modernized society can be understood less as a failure of the compensatory criminal justice system than as an indicator of the growing failure or limits of our society's productive institutions.

In the last century, we have created four great public systems to ensure a productive society. They were designed to provide education, social support, housing, and job training for all Americans, with special provisions for the most vulnerable or disadvantaged. These systems are our public schools, the program of public welfare benefits, the various forms of public housing, and the numerous public job training and employment programs.

Historically, these systems have served effectively to benefit many Americans. However, to the degree that they were intended to create a "safety net" to keep those least advantaged within the productive boundaries of society, they have recently lost their effectiveness. Indeed, they have begun to create effects that are the *opposite* of their intentions. In many low-income areas, the schools, welfare system, housing projects and jobs programs seem to create a web of hopelessness rather than a safety net.

As these great public systems have lost their productive power, the society has responded to people caught in their web with a commitment to more and more human services to fix the lives of those damaged by the failing systems. The rapid growth of these human services has created a large new intervention system in low-income areas. However, this system has nowhere reversed the decline of low-income neighborhoods. It has neither fixed enough lives to make neighborhoods productive nor fixed the failing primary public systems that caused its growth. The human services have, instead, created another system that is now widely understood to be a fifth part of the web of hopelessness.

It is the people, caught in this web of counterproductive systems, who must seek survival in the hopeless spaces available. They react in many ways, just as we would. They strike out in anger, as some of us would. They create productive, phoenix-like new ventures and initiatives, as some of us would. They despair and retreat into addictions, as some of us would. They are normal people in an abnormal world, surrounded by expensive, costly helping systems that are the walls that bound their lives. To defy those walls, they must live abnormal lives—often productive, sometimes destructive, always creative.

Our radical incarceration rate is one of our uncreative and unproductive responses to normal lives forced into abnormal responses to counterproductive systems. To understand how we arrived at this paradoxical situation points toward the policy directions for genuine reform.

Historically, low-income neighborhoods have been sites of struggle and suffering at the margin of society. But they have also been stepping-stones to the center of society. Within the reach of the residents was a way in to prosperity rather than the way out to incarceration.

The way in depended upon two *primary* resources—economic opportunity and the strength of local communities. The safety-net systems were built *under* these resources and would have failed had economy and community not been there. However, these two foundation resources began to erode after World War II.

The neighborhood economy began to dissolve as industrial systems closed down and moved out. The remaining industry suburbanized and the new jobs were services—dead ends or high-tech and white-collar professional. These systems are not stepping-stones, physically or technically, for many people in the lowest-income neighborhoods.

In the place of the eroding industrial system, the human service system grew in the neighborhoods. It provided increasing professional interventions designed to fix and mend those injured in the economic retreat. Although the growing service system was motivated by the best of intentions, it had two unintended side effects with devastating consequences.

First, the service system was actually competing with the primary community problem-solving and support structures: family, relatives, neighbors, block clubs, neighborhood organizations, local associations, churches, ethnic groups, and so on. The hidden message of the service system was that paid professionals are the powerful support providers and problem-solvers. Therefore, community groups need not bother. As the local economy eroded, the obvious wealth of the developing service systems made the professional argument even more powerful. A consequence of the claims of the service system was that comprehensive, coordinated neighborhood service centers often replaced the community groups created by local citizens, thus transforming the local citizens into clients. As clients, they understood well-being as the result of services received rather than as the product of their creative capacity. The ultimate consequence was the growth of client dependence rather than citizen capacity.

The second unintended side effect was the negative economic consequence of the burgeoning human service economy. This system became the principal beneficiary of the government's low-income programs. While neighborhood residents struggled in the face of declining incomes, the remedial programs principally benefited the paid professionals and workers in the service systems—and they were not usually local residents. As a result, by the beginning of the nineties in most cities, over 60 percent of all public program dollars went to service, commodity, and housing providers. The remaining dollars provided meager local incomes that actually represented legislated poverty.

If we are to restore the stepping-stones from low-income neighborhoods into the center of society, we must face these facts:

1. The two foundation stones of reform are economy and community.
2. The human service system can never substitute for these two resources.
3. The great public support systems cannot do their work if the primary foundations are eroded.

For policymakers, the alternative to ever-growing incarceration is clear. First, there must be a relentless focus upon initiatives that regenerate income and work. This regeneration will require relocating many resources from unproductive service systems to economy-enhancing local activities.

Second, there must be a new commitment to enhancing the powers of local associations, churches, and neighborhood organizations as the principal agents of support and problem-solving.

These two standards command a review of all public programs, testing them against these policy principles:

1. Does the public investment increase the income or the economic opportunity of the person of low income?
2. Does the public investment support the local community and its organizations and associations in doing the basic work that needs to be done?

Finally, to act on these principles will require hard choices. We are a society coming to grips with the recognition that our resources are limited. We cannot invest in growing human services and correctional systems while increasing investments in economy and community. Indeed, should we invest ever more in failed service and correctional systems, the economic and community stepping-stones to a viable society will vanish under the rising tide of the waters of hopelessness.

On Community

Community Organizing in the Eighties: Toward a Post-Alinsky Agenda

WITH JOHN KRETZMANN

The legacy of community-organizing giant Saul Alinsky has been central to the continuing emergence of a diverse "neighborhood movement" since the 1940s. While skilled and inventive organizers have seldom regarded Alinsky's approaches as divinely inspired, many have continued to work in communities as if the master's most basic assumptions about the nature of neighborhoods and the logic of organizing strategies were more or less immutable.

Reflecting on the actual experience of activist neighborhood organizations in recent years, we want to suggest, first, that the structure of poor and working-class urban neighborhoods has changed since Alinsky first began organizing in Chicago's Back of the Yards nearly fifty years ago; and, second, that given these changes in neighborhoods, a number of the classic Alinsky strategies and tactics are in need of critical revision (which, of course, many good organizers already know).

For Alinsky and his disciples, the city was reducible to two basic units: the neighborhood and the "enemy" outside the

neighborhood. Poor and working-class neighborhoods contin-
ually suffered because external decision-makers controlled the
internal distribution of services and goods. Foreshadowing
more recent analyses of neighborhoods as units of "collective
consumption," Alinsky's approach essentially argued for the
building of the first modern consumer organizations—in this
case, defined by geography.

Two further assumptions about the nature of neighborhoods
and their "enemies" or "targets" shaped the basic Alinsky strategy. First, the neighborhood contained within it a number of
vital organizations, even though they were not "organized" to
act as a unit. Four basic kinds of associations were particularly
important—churches, ethnic groups, political organizations,
and labor unions. The organizer's task was to forge a coalition
of leaders from these groups. Their constituencies would then
follow as the "organization of organizations" model took
shape. Because of this existing pattern of associations, organizers could concentrate on pulling together their leaders, a very
small percentage of the neighborhood's residents, and could
plausibly claim representative community status for their new
neighborhood group.

The second set of assumptions behind Alinsky's strategy
concerned the enemy, or target, and focused on three interre-
lated characteristics. A target, the strategically defined embodiment of the causes of a neighborhood problem, was thought
to be: (a) *visible*, and therefore concretely definable; (b) *local*,
and therefore accessible; and (c) *capable*, and therefore pos-
sessed of the resources and authority to correct the problem.

In summary, then, the basic Alinsky approach emphasized
organizing in the consumer mode by assembling preexisting
organizations into a kind of dense pack and propelling this
aggregate toward a visible local decision-making structure to
force it to do what the neighborhood wanted. For many years,
this model of Alinsky-type organizing both reflected accurately the nature of city neighborhoods and, more important,
got results.

Today, however, conditions have changed dramatically in most working-class and poor urban neighborhoods, where the rates of active participation of residents in at least three of the four organizational building blocks seem to have declined. As Walter Dean Burnham and others have pointed out, local identification with and participation in political parties is diminishing. The shrinkage of the older industrial labor unions, combined with the general centralization and professionalization of their staffs, has blunted their local influence. In many cities, the dispersion of second- and third-generation ethnics from their neighborhoods of origin has significantly loosened the bonds of ethnic solidarity. In this context, the fact that a number of organizing networks depend increasingly on the local churches for their base becomes totally understandable.

Further explanations for this decline in organized local participation abound. Higher job and residency mobility rates are often the result of the growing marginalization of the secondary labor market upon which so many of these neighborhoods depend. Local housing markets continue to be manipulated by real estate interests. Changes in the family economy have dramatically increased the number of women in the labor force, with a consequent decrease in voluntary activity. Perhaps most significantly, the long-term trend toward the separation of workplace from residence has continued unchecked. (In this connection, it is important to recall that Alinsky's initial conceptions of community organizing reflected a direct attempt to translate his labor-organizing experience with the CIO into a context defined by residency. Today, it is increasingly difficult for the workplace to "teach" the home.)

If neighborhoods themselves have changed significantly, so too have the "targets" of community organizations. Simply put, it has become nearly impossible to identify targets that are visible, local, and capable.

First, targets are not visible and tangible in poor and working-class neighborhoods because they are no longer there.

On the entire West Side of Chicago, as well as in old Alinsky-organized neighborhoods like Woodlawn, almost no banking institutions remain—nor do many plants, factories, or retailing or wholesaling operations. (This is, of course, what is meant by disinvestment.)

Second, in those neighborhoods where major economic institutions do remain visible, they are clearly not local. Instead, they are local expressions of large corporations. Accelerating centralization and consolidation of control across economic sectors have left local managers marginal pawns in the high-stakes games run from headquarters in a few rebuilt downtowns. Effects of economic decisions on neighborhoods themselves are not even a part of the headquarters calculations. It is in this light that neighborhood conditions are understood as "residual" rather than direct results of capital movement and investment policies. By now, it is clear that neighborhoods as well as entire municipalities are attaining this dubious residual status. As one Midwestern banker put it, "I can't do a thing locally. Now we're just a branch city."

Third, those institutions that remain both visible and local in poor and working-class neighborhoods are precisely those publicly funded service agencies that are least capable of producing results no matter how hard a community organization confronts them. More and more organizers have come to recognize that neighborhood security, for example, is no longer a function of the numbers of police present. Others have seen that large school bureaucracies are often ineffective in improving education no matter what their intentions.

Therefore, today's community organizers cannot assume that either their assumptions about local structures or the tactics handed down from earlier generations are appropriate to the kinds of neighborhoods in which they work today. What is needed is a heightened commitment to exploration and invention at the neighborhood level—experiments that adapt the classic Alinsky model to drastically changed conditions.

What might these experiments look like? To this question

we can offer some tentative responses—new directions based primarily on conversations with organizers themselves, and coming out of their own problems and experiments in neighborhoods.

In the kinds of neighborhoods we are concerned about, it becomes less and less likely that strategies stressing either the consolidation of existing associations or the confronting of an outside enemy make much sense. Socially atomized and increasingly cut off from centralized, unresponsive mainstream economic institutions, these neighborhoods and their residents present a new challenge to organizers.

It seems clear that new strategies must stress an organizing process that enhances and builds community, and that focuses on developing a neighborhood's own capacities to do for itself what outsiders will or can no longer do. Taking neighborhoods seriously in their current condition means building social, political, and economic structures at the local level that re-create a space for these people to act and decide.

This shift involves, first of all, a reconceptualization of neighborhood as a locus for production as well as consumption. Organizations originally oriented to the goal of equalizing consumption patterns between and within neighborhoods are increasingly turning toward an agenda that centers on building internal neighborhood productive capacities. With this shift comes a parallel reorientation of strategy—from organizing confrontation over service distribution issues to organizing confrontation over production and the resources necessary to produce.

Experimenting with this new agenda for community-building has focused some organizers on three different centers of activity: the local neighborhood, the public sector, and the private sector.

First, within the neighborhood itself, taking production and community-building seriously involves:

1. Continuing to push the good work in commercial, industrial, and housing development already begun by
   large numbers of local development corporations in
   the last decade.
2. Expanding greatly the number of cooperative, neigh-
   borhood-owned, worker-owned, and joint-venture
   enterprises for the production of both exportable and
   locally useful goods. As technologies develop and
   economies of scale reach and surpass their limits, food
   and energy production, waste management, and other
   enterprises dealing with the basics of life may in fact be
   more usefully efficient and economically pursued at
   the local level.
3. Similarly, community-based and -owned enterprises in
   the still-expanding services and communications areas
   need further exploration. Neither service contracts nor
   the implements of the "wired community," replete
   with cable TV and interactive microcomputers, need
   be owned and controlled by outsiders.

Second, an agenda centered on building local productive
capacities requires new relationships with public sector bodies
so that both resources and real authority are transferred to the
neighborhood. Such an approach involves:

1. Taking a thorough look at the public dollars already
   being spent in the neighborhood and devising strategies aimed at shifting their uses away from traditional
   transfer and maintenance functions toward investment
   approaches.
2. Developing strategies designed to direct public resources to neighborhood development groups. For in-
   stance, organizations might work toward a version of a
   "neighborhood checkoff" program, in which the city is
   persuaded to return a small percentage of a neighborhood's taxes to the local neighborhood organization.
   Each household would be entitled to a "chit," which

could be expended with the neighborhood organization of its choice.

3. A variety of neighborhood-based forms of governance carrying significant local authority. Such bodies are emerging in a variety of shapes in a number of cities. Admittedly, the task of tailoring their jurisdiction to the particular needs of a neighborhood remains a tricky one. But without increased local authority, neighborhood strategies will be forced to remain primarily reactive.

Third, and most difficult, any serious approach to community-building *must* devise ways to reroot business, to insert locality into the equations by which businesses make decisions. This is a national, even international, policy agenda, calling for a coalition politics that we have not seen in recent years. However, without the successful pursuit of such an agenda, any movement toward building local productive capacities will remain peripheral to the ever-increasing mobility of both producers and capital. The directions in which this agenda might move are already emerging from a variety of networks across the country, and might be seen as embracing two connected strategies:

1. Organizations might agree upon the basic outlines of a "Corporate Accountability Act" that would provide a variety of incentives and penalties related to the needs of communities for jobs and location commitments as well as local representation on boards or regulatory bodies. Such an act would incorporate the most universal elements of current and pending plant-closing legislation, and could model itself on the organizational groundwork laid by the Community Reinvestment Act, which requires financial institutions to invest in older neighborhoods.

2. Concurrently, organizations might agree to pursue something like a "Community Banking Act," designed

to define the obligations of financial institutions for local credit allocation. It has become dismayingly clear that the local availability of low-interest, long-term money from local savings institutions and other sources has all but dried up in most neighborhoods, and that local borrowers now compete directly with the United States government, United States Steel, and the government of Brazil for investment capital. Reestablishing the very existence of a local credit market is essential for the community-building agenda.

Taken together, these initial suggestions define the emerging shape of a post-Alinsky agenda for urban neighborhoods. They argue for an organizing approach aimed at building community through the restoration of localized political economies.

To join politics and economics at the neighborhood level is to do both an old and a new thing. Analyzing "political economy," after all, was what both Adam Smith and Karl Marx thought they were about. But reigning orthodoxies have succeeded in segregating economics from politics in both theory and practice. In our neighborhoods we have often practiced politics as if economics didn't exist, and economics as if politics didn't matter. The practice of either is diminished by the absence of its counterpart. Even wise and committed neighborhood commentators tell us about "neighborhood government" *or* "neighborhood economy," perpetuating the compartmentalization.

But effective organizers are learning quickly that restoring the practice of an economics in which place matters, and in which production builds rather than destroys community, involves a major political challenge. We can only imagine that if Alinsky himself were still around to growl his advice at us, he would admonish us to take up that challenge while we still have neighborhoods left to build.

Regenerating Community

Each of us has a map of the social world in our mind, and the way we act, our plans and opinions, are the result of that map.

The people who make social policy also have social maps in their minds. They make plans and design programs based upon their maps. Indeed, if you carefully examine their programs, you can detect the nature of their mental maps.

Using this method, we have found that the most common social policy map has two locations: institutions and individual people. By institutions we mean large structures such as corporations, universities, and government mental health systems. These structures organize a large group of people so that a few of them will be able to control the rest of them. In this structure, there is ultimately room for one leader. It is a structure initially created to produce goods such as steel and automobiles.

Since the 1930s, the structure has also been used to design human service systems. While these newly designed hierarchical, managed service systems do not produce goods such as steel, they do produce needs assessments, service plans, protocols, and procedures. They are also thought by some policymakers to produce health, education, security, or justice.

If it is correct that these systems can produce these service commodities, then it is possible to imagine that there are consumers of their products. For example, we have all heard that there are now people called "health consumers." They are the *individuals* who are the other part of the social map created by most social policymakers. They make a complete economic world by acting as the users (consumers) of the products of managed institutional producers of such commodities as mental health, health, education, and justice. Thus, we can see that it was necessary to create health consumers once we had systems that could produce health. Otherwise, there would be no purpose for these large hierarchical, managed systems. Once we understand this social map of institutions and individuals, we can see why we have mental health providers and mental health consumers. We can also see how our developing service economy works.

Because the gross national product is the sum of the goods and *services* produced each year, many policy experts have come to believe that the well-being of our society increasingly depends upon the amount of the commodities called services that are produced by institutions and used by consumers. For example, a person with a perilous and extended illness (a health consumer) contributes significantly to our economic growth by using large amounts of the commodities produced by the health system. Indeed, a very ill person disabled for a considerable amount of time could cause production of much more medical dollar value through their illness than the value of their own production were they healthy.

This amazing development is possible, in part, because of the unusual two-place map used by many social policymakers in designing social service programs. Unfortunately, this map and the program designs that flow from it have recently encountered three major problems.

The first problem is that in spite of ever-growing inputs into institutionalized service systems, many individuals continue to reject their roles as consumers. This is the problem of intractability that has resulted in an increasing focus upon the "compliance" issue. Especially in our big cities, many intractable young individuals continue to refuse to learn in spite of heightened resources and managerial inputs to school systems. This is commonly known as the educational problem.

Similarly, there are many other intractable individuals who refuse to behave in spite of our correctional institutions. This is the crime problem. There is also the nutrition problem, created by intractable people who refuse to eat the right food. And the chemical dependency problem created by intractable people who insist on smoking and drinking incorrectly. There is also the ever-growing number of intractable people who refuse to flourish in institutions created for labeled people, in spite of all the professional and managerial improvements designed by the systems.

Indeed, there are so many intractable people refusing to consume institutional services that we are now creating new megasystems designed to surround these individuals with professionally administered services. Thus, one can now see individuals whose lives are bounded by institutions "targeting" their services at an intractable individual through teachers, doctors, trainers, social workers, family planners, psychologists, vocational counselors, security officers, and so forth. This is usually called a "comprehensive, multidisciplinary, coordinated, interagency 'wrap-around' service system." It is the equivalent of institutionalization without walls or the design of an environment to create a totally dependent service system consumer.

The second problem with programs based upon the typical social policy map is that the sum of their costs can be greater than the wealth of the nation. In a recent white paper entitled "A Time to Serve," a group of Swedish government planners described the escalating costs of their much-acclaimed social service system. They point out that at present rates of growth, the system could consume the entire nation's wealth within a few decades. Therefore, they propose that the government begin to "tax" people's time by requiring the Swedish people to contribute unpaid work to the maintenance and growth of their social service system.

While it is clearly the case that the United States is not in immediate danger of the Swedish economic dilemma, we are contributing substantial amounts to social service systems. A 1984 study by the Community Services Society of New York found that approximately $7,000 per capita of public and private money is specifically allocated to the low-income population of that city. Thus, a family of four would be eligible on a per capita basis for $28,000, which would place them in the moderate-income category. However, only 37 percent of this money actually reaches low-income people in cash income. Nearly two-thirds is consumed by those who service the poor.

The third problem with the typical social policy map is that programs based upon its suppositions are increasingly ineffective and even counterproductive. For example, we now understand that our "correctional systems" consistently train people in crime. Studies demonstrate that a substantial number of people, while in hospitals, become sick or injured with maladies worse than those for which they were admitted. In many of our big-city schools we see children whose relative achievement levels fall farther behind each year. Thus, we have come to recognize the possibility that we can create crime-making corrections systems, sickness-making health systems, and stupid-making schools based upon a social model that conceives of society as a place bounded by institutions and individuals.

It is obvious, upon the briefest reflection, that the typical social policy map is inaccurate because it excludes a major social domain—the community. By community, we mean the social place used by family, friends, neighbors, neighborhood associations, clubs, civic groups, local enterprises, churches, ethnic associations, synagogues, local unions, local government, and local media. In addition to being called the community, this social environment is also described as the informal sector, the unmanaged environment, and the associational sector.

The Struggle Between Community and Institution

These associations of the community represent unique social tools that are unlike the social tool represented by a managed institution. For example, the structure of institutions is a design established to create *control* of people. On the other hand, the structure of associations is the result of people acting through *consent*. It is critical that we distinguish between these two motivating forces because there are many goals that can be fulfilled only through consent, and these are often goals that will be impossible to achieve through a production system designed to control.

There are many other unique characteristics of the community of associations:

- The associations in community are interdependent. To weaken one is to weaken all. If the local newspaper closes, the garden club and the township meeting will each diminish as they lose a voice. If the American Legion disbands, several community fund-raising events and the maintenance of the ballpark will stop. If the Baptist church closes, several self-help groups that meet in the basement will be without a home and folks in the old people's home will lose their weekly visitors. The interdependence of associations and the dependence of community upon their work is the vital center of an effective society.
- The community environment is constructed around the recognition of fallibility rather than the ideal. Most institutions, on the other hand, are designed with a vision imagining a structure where things can be done right, a kind of orderly perfection achieved, and the ablest dominate.
- In contrast, community structures tend to proliferate until they create a place for everyone, no matter how fallible. They provide vehicles that give voice to diversity and assume that consensual contribution is the primary value.

- In the proliferation of community associations, there is room for many leaders and the development of leadership capacity among many. This democratic opportunity structure assumes that the best idea is the sum of the knowledge of the collected fallible people who are citizens. Indeed, it is the marvel of the democratic ideal that people of every fallibility are citizens. Effective associational life incorporates all of those fallibilities and reveals the unique intelligence of community.
- Associations have the capacity to respond quickly. They do not need to involve all of the institutional interests incorporated in a planning committee, budget office, administrative staff, and so forth.
- A primary characteristic of people who need help is that their problem is created by the unexpected tragedy, the surprise development, the sudden change. While they will be able to stabilize over the long run, what they often need is immediate help. The rapid response capacity of associations and their interconnectedness allow for the possibility of immediate and comprehensive assistance without first initiating a person into a system from which he or she may never leave.
- The proliferation and development of community associations allow for the flowering of creative solutions. Institutions tend to require creative ideas to follow channels. However, the nonhierarchical nature of the field of associations allows us to see all of the budding ideas and greatly increases our opportunities for social innovation.
- Because community associations are small, face-to-face groups, the relationship among members is very individualized. They also have the tradition of dealing with nonmembers as individuals. Institutions, on the other hand, have great difficulty developing programs or activities that recognize the unique characteristics of each individual. Therefore, associations represent unusual tools for

creating "hand-tailored" responses to those who may be in special need or have unique fallibilities.

- Our institutions are constantly reforming and reorganizing themselves in an effort to create or allow relationships that can be characterized as "care." Nonetheless, their ministrations consistently commodify themselves and become a service. For many people with uncommon fallibilities, their need is for care rather than service. While a managed system organized as a structure of control can deliver a service, it cannot deliver care. Care is a special relationship characterized by consent rather than control. Therefore, its auspices are individual and associational. For those who need care, we must recognize the community as the appropriate social tool.

- Finally, associations and the community they create are the forum within which citizenship can be expressed. Institutions by their managed structure are definitionally unable to act as forums for citizenship. Therefore, the vital center of democracy is the community of associations. Any person without access to that forum is effectively denied citizenship. For those people with unique fallibilities who have been institutionalized, it is not enough that they be deinstitutionalized. In order to be citizens, they must also have the opportunity for recommunalization.

In summary, the community of associations provides a social tool in which consent is the primary motivation, interdependence creates wholistic environments, people of all capacities and fallibilities are incorporated, quick responses are possible, creativity is multiplied rather than channeled, individualized responses are characteristic, care is able to replace service, and citizenship is possible. When all of these unique capacities of community are recognized, it is obvious why the social policy map that excludes community life has resulted in increasing failures. To exclude from our problem-solving capacities the social tool of community is to have taken the heart out of America.

Why is it, then, that social policy maps so often ignore community? One reason is that there are many institutional leaders who simply do not believe in the capacities of communities. They often see communities as collections of parochial, inexpert, uninformed, and biased people. Indeed, there are many leaders of service systems who believe that they are in direct competition with communities for the power to correctly define problems and provide scientific solutions and professional services.

In this competitive understanding, the institutional leaders are correct. Whenever hierarchical systems become more powerful than the community, we see the flow of authority, resources, skills, dollars, legitimacy, and capacities away from communities to service systems. In fact, institutionalized systems grow at the expense of communities. As institutions gain power, communities lose their potency and the consent of community is replaced by the control of systems; the care of community is replaced by the service of systems; the citizens of community are replaced by the clients and consumers of institutional products.

Visions of Society

Today, our society is the site of the struggle between community and institution for the capacities and loyalties of our people. This struggle is never carried out in the abstract. Instead, it occurs each day in the relations of people, the budget decisions of systems, and the public portraits of the media. As one observes this struggle, there appear to be three visions of society that dominate the discourse.

The first is the *therapeutic vision.* This prospect sees the well-being of individuals as growing from an environment composed of professionals and their services. It envisions a world where there is a professional to meet every need, and where the fee to secure each professional service is a right. This vision is epigrammatically expressed by those who see the ultimate liberty as "the right to treatment."

The second prospect is the *advocacy vision*. This approach foresees a world in which labeled people will be in an environment protected by advocates and advocacy groups. It conceives an individual whose world is guarded by legal advocates, support people, job developers, and housing locaters. Unlike the therapeutic vision, the advocacy approach conceives a defensive wall of helpers to protect an individual against an alien community. It seeks to ensure a person's right to be a functioning individual.

The third approach is the *community vision*. It sees the goal as "recommunalization" of exiled and labeled individuals. It understands the community as the basic context for enabling people to contribute their gifts. It sees community associations as contexts in which to create and locate jobs, provide opportunities for recreation and multiple friendships, and become the political defender of the right of labeled people to be free from exile.

Those who seek to institute the community vision believe that beyond therapy and advocacy is the constellation of community associations. They see a society where those who were once labeled, exiled, treated, counseled, advised, and protected are, instead, incorporated into community, where their contributions, capacities, gifts, and fallibilities will allow a network of relationships involving work, recreation, friendship, support, and the political power of being a citizen.

Because so many labeled people have been exiled to a world expressing the therapeutic and advocacy vision of an appropriate life, the community vision has frequently been forgotten. How will people know when they are in community? Our studies suggest that this universe is distinctive and distinguished from the environment of systems and institutions.

The community experience incorporates a number of strands.

Capacity. We all remember the childhood question regarding how to describe a glass with water to its midpoint. Is it half-full or half-empty? Community associations are built upon the recognition of the fullness of each member because it is the sum of his or her capacities that represents the power of the group. The social policy mapmakers, on the other hand, build a world based upon the emptiness of each of us—a model based upon deficiency and need. Communities depend upon capacities. Systems commodify deficiencies.

Collective effort. It is obvious that the essence of community is people working together. One of the characteristics of this community work is shared responsibility that requires many talents. Thus, a person who has been labeled deficient can find a "hammock" of support in the collective capacities of a community that can shape itself to the unique character of each person. This collective process contrasts with the individualistic approach of the therapeutic professional and the rigidity of institutions that demand that people shape themselves to the needs of the system.

Informality. Associational life in the community is a critical element of the informal economy. Here transactions of value take place without money, advertising, or hype. Authentic relationships are possible and care emerges in place of its packaged imitation: service.

The informality of community is also expressed through relationships that are not managed. Communities viewed by those who understand only managed experiences and relationships appear to be disordered, messy, and inefficient. What these people fail to understand is that there is a hidden order to community groups that is determined by the need to incorporate capacity and fallibility.

While institutions and professionals war against human fallibility by trying to replace it, cure it, or disregard it, communities are proliferations of associations that multiply until they incorporate both the capacities and the fallibilities of citizens.

It is for this reason that labeled people are not out of place in community because they all have capacities and only their fallibilities are unusual. However, because there are so many community associations, there are always some sets of associational relationships that can incorporate their fallibilities and use their unique gifts.

Stories. In universities, people know through studies. In businesses and bureaucracies, people know by reports. In communities, people know by stories. These community stories allow people to reach back into their common history and their individual experience for knowledge about truth and direction for the future.

Professionals and institutions often threaten the stories of community by urging community people to count up things rather than communicate. Successful community associations resist efforts to impose the foreign language of studies and reports because it is a tongue that ignores their own capacities and insights. Whenever communities come to believe that their common knowledge is illegitimate, they lose their power and professionals and systems rapidly invade their social place.

Celebration. Community groups constantly incorporate celebrations, parties, and social events into their activities. The line between work and play is blurred and the human nature of everyday life becomes part of the way of work. You will know that you are in community if you often hear laughter and singing. You will know you are in an institution, a corporation, or a bureaucracy if you hear the silence of long halls and reasoned meetings. Associations in community celebrate because they work by consent and have the luxury of allowing joyfulness to join them in their endeavors.

Tragedy. The surest indication of the experience of community is the explicit common knowledge of tragedy, death, and suffering. The managed, ordered, technical vision embodied in professional and institutional systems leaves no space for tragedy; they are basically methods for production. Indeed, they are designed to deny the central dilemmas of life. Therefore, our managed systems gladly give communities the real dilemmas of the human condition. There is no competition here. To be in community is to be an active part of associations and self-help groups. To be in community is to be a part of ritual, lamentation, and celebration of our fallibility.

Knowing community is not an abstract understanding. Rather, it is what we each know about all of us.

As we think about ourselves, our community, and our institutions, many of us recognize that we have been degraded because our roles as citizens and our communities have been traded for the right to clienthood and consumer status. Many of us have come to recognize that as we exiled our fallible neighbors to the control of managers, therapists, and technicians, we lost much of our power to be the vital center of society. We forgot about the capacity of every single one of us to do good work and, instead, made some of us into the objects of good works—servants of those who serve. As we think about our community life, we recognize that something has happened to many of us as institutions have grown in power: We have become too impotent to be called real citizens and too disconnected to be effective members of community.

There is a mistaken notion that our society has a problem in terms of effective human services. Our essential problem is weak communities. While we have reached the limits of institutional problem-solving, we are only at the beginning of exploring the possibility of a new vision for community. It is a vision of regeneration. It is a vision of reassociating the exiled. It is a vision of freeing ourselves from service and advocacy. It is a vision of centering our lives in community.

We all know that community must be the center of our lives because it is only in community that we can be citizens. It is only in community that we can find care. It is only in community that we can hear people singing. And if you listen carefully, you can hear the words: "I care for you, because you are mine, and I am yours."

Christian Service

On the Backwardness of Prophets

A friend recently told me that a prophet is someone who has everything backwards.

That observation is correct in terms of dissenting prophets. Traditionally, they are people, like Jeremiah, who assert old values and oppose the order of the day. Their prophetic voice says to us, "You have it backwards." We, of course, believe that the prophet has it backwards and continue in our errant ways.

There are, however, some modern prophets who present a contrast. While they were people who had it backwards, they went beyond their prophecy and led people in revolutions that reordered the world. They not only had it backwards, they also reversed the order. Two modern examples are Thomas Jefferson and Gandhi. Each had it backwards in the traditional prophetic sense. But each also led a revolution to reverse the order—to get things straight. While these two were unusual prophets in that they acted as well as predicted, they were unique because after their revolutions, they *still* had it backwards.

After the American Revolution, Thomas Jefferson was convinced that our new society most needed the opportunity to overthrow itself. He still had it backwards.

Gandhi led the Indian people into the independence of the modern world and then urged them to use the ancient hand spinning wheel as the ultimate expression of capacity and freedom. He still had it backwards.

In traditional terms, Jesus was a prophet who had it backwards. He said that the poor, not the rich, will inherit the Kingdom. He said it was the hungry who would be satisfied. He said those who weep will be those who laugh.

While He had it backwards in the traditional sense, would He, like Jefferson and Gandhi, still have it backwards after the Christian revolution?

The traditional summation of Christ's reversal of the given order has been defined by Christians as the imperative to be a servant—*not* a lord. The highest vision of the Christian purpose is to reverse the order, to fulfill a mission of service. We serve Christ by following His example in washing the feet of the disciples. We are Christians, people who have it backwards, as we serve rather than rule—act as servants rather than lords.

There is a problem, however, with our dedication to service as the ultimate Christian ideal. After all, the Crusaders thought they were servants of Christ. We doubt it today.

The conquistadors thought they were servants of Christ. We doubt it today.

The missionaries who went to Africa and Asia thought they were servants of Christ. But many doubt even that today.

It is clear, then, that many people called Christian servants did not reverse the order. They didn't really have it backwards. Instead, they used the idea of servanthood to conquer, rule, and dominate others in Christ's name. They had Christ backwards.

It is not enough, therefore, to ask whether someone *says* he or she is serving Christ. There are bad servants and good servants. The critical issue may be understanding the difference. A good servant must really have it backwards. She can't use the Christian imperatives of mission and service to dominate and control.

Today it seems much easier to distinguish the good servants from the bad. Because of McCarthyism, Vietnam, and Watergate, we know that modern Crusaders, conquistadors, and missionaries can be bad servants.

Our current good servants seem clearly to help, care, and cure rather than conquer, exploit, and control. Our good servants are doctors, teachers, psychologists, social workers, professors, lawyers, counselors—the professionals who serve.

Our society has even made these good servants, the helping professionals, the economic base of the nation. In GNP terms, nearly two-thirds of our employed people now produce services. We have become an economy of servants. Instead of a nation of conquistadors, we are a nation of servers. The economic proof is that in 1976 we spent $119 billion for "defense" but more than $138 billion for only one service—medicine.

As Christians we could celebrate the institutionalization of the good servant. Ours is finally a society of caring, helping, curing servanthood. We laud the value of professional servanthood and pay for it generously.

In our society of servants, it is interesting to consider what Christ might see with all His tendency toward getting things backwards. Would He, like Jefferson and Gandhi, still have it backwards? Would He even reject a society of good servants?

The answer is, probably not, unless He saw good servants becoming lords. Probably not, unless He saw help becoming control, care becoming commercialized, and cure becoming immobilizing. On the other hand, if He found servants involved in commercialized, immobilizing systems of control, He would certainly insist that we still have it backwards—that our servanthood had become lordship.

The question, then, is whether we are a nation of good servants or the lords of commercialized, immobilizing systems of service that actually control.

Consider modern universities as institutions serving students. We might ask whether they have become commercial gatekeepers whose grades select the elites who will control the future. Are professors people who convince eighteen-year-olds, and the rest of society, that young people are incompetent beings in need of technical infusions that will enable their deficient selves to be effective agents in serving systems? Are professors servants who depend upon deficiency and control rather than competence and community?

If faculty members are gatekeepers of commerce depending upon deficiency and control, they are surely bad servants—modern conquistadors. Their servanthood would then be lordship and they would have inverted Christ's mandate to serve. Once again, He would certainly have it backwards, and insist that they have made the servant the lord.

I wonder whether the human reality is always to make servanthood into lordship. It may be that there is no way to define service so that we will not get it backwards and make it a system of control. With all our Christian devotion to the idea of service, could service be an inadequate ideal—a value so easily corrupted that we should question its usefulness?

At the Last Supper, Christ was telling the disciples those things of greatest importance. It was His final opportunity to communicate the central values of the faith. In St. John's report of Christ's concluding instruction, Christ said, "No longer do I call you servants, for the servant does not know what the master is doing. I call you friends for all that I have heard from my Father, I have made known to you."

Finally, Christ said you are *not* servants. You *know*. You are *friends*.

Perhaps beyond the revolution of Christian service is the final revolution, the possibility of being friends. Friends are people who *know*, care, respect, struggle, love justice, and have a commitment to each other through time.

Friends are people who understand that it is not servants—the professors, lawyers, doctors, and teachers—who make God's world. Rather, friends are people who understand that it is through their mutual action that they become Christians.

Christ's mandate to be friends is a revolutionary idea in our serving society. Here we are, a nation of professionalized servers, following Christ's mandate to serve. And here He is, at the final moment, getting it backwards once again. The final message is not to serve. Rather, He directs us to be friends.

Why friends rather than servants? Perhaps it is because He knew that servants could always become lords but that friends could not. Servants are people who *know the mysteries* that can control those to whom they give "help." Friends are people who *know each other.* They are free to give *and* receive help.

In our time, professionalized servants are people who are limited by the unknowing friendlessness of their help.

Friends, on the other hand, are people liberated by the possibilities of knowing how to help each other.

Notes

The Professional Problem

1. Ivan Illich, *Medical Nemesis* (New York: Pantheon, 1976).

2. Peter Berger and Richard Neuhaus, *To Empower People: The Role of Mediating Structures in Public Policy* (Washington, D.C.: American Enterprise Institute for Public Policy Research, 1977).

3. Eli Ginzberg, "The Professionalization of the U.S. Labor Force," *Scientific American* (March 1979): 48–53.

4. Jacques Barzun, "The Professions Under Siege," *Harpers* (October 1978): 61–68.

5. Nathan Glazer, "The Attack on the Professions," *Commentary* (November 1978): 34–41.

6. See Illich, *Medical Nemesis*.

7. See Berger and Neuhaus, *To Empower People*.

8. Christopher Lasch, *Haven in a Heartless World* (New York: Basic Books, 1977).

9. See Barzun, "The Professions."

Diagnosis and the Health of Community

1. Victor R. Fuchs, "A Tale of Two States," in *The Sociology of Health and Illness*, ed. Peter Conrad (New York: St. Martin's Press, 1990).

2. Rene Dubos, *The Mirage of Health* (New York: Harper, 1959).

3. Dianne Kallenback and Arthur Lyons, *Government Spending for the Poor in Cook County* (Evanston, Ill.: Center for Urban Affairs and Policy Research, Northwestern University, 1989).

4. Figures 1 and 2 are from a report titled *Mapping Community Capacity* (Evanston, Ill.: Center for Urban Affairs and Policy Research, Northwestern University).

A Nation of Clients?

1. Victor R. Fuchs, *The Growing Importance of the Service Industries*, Occasional Paper 96 (New York: National Bureau of Economic Research, 1965).

2. Daniel Bell, *The Coming of the Post Industrial Society* (New York: Basic Books, 1973).

3. Daniel Bell, "The Coming of the Post Industrial Society," *TWA Ambassador* (January 1976).

4. American Bar Association, *A Review of Legal Education in the United States* (Chicago: American Bar Association, 1979); see also American Bar Association, *Membership Report* (Chicago: American Bar Association, 1980).

5. Nancy Phillipi, "Income Maintenance Project" (Evanston, Ill.: Center for Urban Affairs, Northwestern University, 1980, mimeographed).

Do No Harm

1. Executive Office of the President, *Up from Dependency*, Supplement 1, Volume 1 (Washington, D.C.: GPO, 1986), reports the major increases between 1960 and 1985 in public allocations to service systems for low-income populations.

2. For the seminal analysis of modern therapeutic counterproductivity, see Ivan Illich, *Medical Nemesis* (New York: Pantheon, 1976).

3. Wolf Wolfensberger, *The Origin and Nature of Our Institutional Models* (Syracuse, N.Y.: Human Policy Press, 1975).

4. Mary O'Connell, *The Gift of Hospitality* (Evanston, Ill.: Center for Urban Affairs and Policy Research, Northwestern University, 1988), is a report of local initiatives designed to counteract this iatrogenic effect in the lives of people labeled developmentally disabled.

5. While commodity programs and vouchers such as food stamps and housing vouchers represent a minority of these dollars, they are often preferable to human service allocations because they provide a greater range of choice and are appropriated for more basic life requirements.

6. Executive Office of the President, *Up from Dependency*, pp. 12–14.

7. David Grossman and Geraldine Smolka, *New York City's Poverty Budget* (New York: Community Service Society of New York, 1984); Diane Kallenback and Arthur Lyons, *Government Spending for the Poor in Cook County, Illinois: Can We Do Better?* (Evanston, Ill.: Center for Urban Affairs and Policy Research, Northwestern University, 1989).

8. Ivan Illich et al., *Disabling Professions* (London: Marion Boyars, 1977).

9. O'Connell, *The Gift of Hospitality.*

10. John McKnight, *The Future of Low-Income Neighborhoods and the People Who Reside There* (Evanston, Ill.: Center for Urban Affairs and Policy Research, Northwestern University, 1987).

11. For example, see David J. Rothman, *The Discovery of the Asylum* (Boston: Little, Brown, 1971).

12. Robert Woodson, *A Summons to Life* (Cambridge, Mass.: Ballinger, 1981).

Redefining Community

1. The Center for Urban Affairs and Policy Research has developed a guide to finding and mapping local associations in your own area called *Getting Connected.* It is available from the Publications Department, Center for Urban Affairs and Policy

Research, Northwestern University, 2040 Sheridan Road, Evanston, IL 60208-4100.

2. For a vivid description of one person who escaped the world of service, see the article by Patrick Worth, president of Ontario People First, in *The Association for the Severely Handicapped (TASH) Newsletter* 15, no. 5 (May 1989): 1–3.

3. Two reports of the work of community guides, *The Gift of Hospitality* and *Community Building in Logan Square*, are available from the Center for Urban Affairs and Policy Research.

4. In an effort to assist policymakers in large public and private agencies to examine their resource allocation from this perspective, we have developed a guide to creating an Environmental Budget, which distinguishes between dollars spent on deficiency-oriented services and dollars focused on the maintenance and expansion of community opportunities. *An Accounting System Designed to Monitor the Environments We Invest in for Labeled People* is available from the Center for Urban Affairs and Policy Research.

Acknowledgments

Grateful acknowledgment is made for permission to reprint the following:

"John Deere and the Bereavement Counselor" reprinted with permission from the E. F. Schumacher Society, Box 76, RD 3, Great Barrington, MA 01230. First presented at the Fourth Annual E. F. Schumacher Lectures.

"The Professional Problem" reprinted with permission from *Institutions,* Journal of the National Center on Institutions and Alternatives, 1979, Volume 2, Number 9.

"The Need for Oldness" reprinted with permission from *The St. Croix Review,* February 1979, Volume 10, Number 1, pp. 22–31.

"Professionalized Service and Disabling Help" reprinted with permission of Marion Boyars Publishers, London and New York, 1977, from *Disabling Professions,* pp. 69–91.

"The Medicalization of Politics" copyright 1975 Christian Century Foundation. Reprinted by permission from the September 17, 1975, issue of *The Christian Century.*

"Well-Being: The New Threshold to the Old Medicine" reprinted with permission from *Health Promotion,* 1986, Volume 1, Number 1, pp. 77–80.

"Diagnosis and the Health of Community" reprinted with permission of the author. Copyright 1992 John McKnight.

"Politicizing Health Care" reprinted with permission from *Social Policy*, November/December 1978, Volume 9, Number 3, pp. 36–39.

"A Nation of Clients?" reprinted with permission from *Public Welfare*, Fall 1980, Volume 38, Number 4, pp. 15–19.

"Do No Harm" reprinted with permission from *Social Policy*, Summer 1989, Volume 20, Number 1, pp. 5–14.

"Redefining Community" reprinted with permission from *Social Policy*, Fall–Winter 1992, Volume 23, Number 2, pp. 56–62.

"A Reconsideration of the Crisis of the Welfare State" reprinted with permission from *Social Policy*, Summer 1985, Volume 16, Number 1, pp. 27–30.

"Thinking About Crime, Sacrifice, and Community" reprinted with permission from *Augustus: A Journal of Progressive Human Services*, 1986, Volume 9, Number 8.

"Community Organizing in the Eighties: Toward a Post-Alinsky Agenda" by John L. McKnight and John P. Kretzmann. Reprinted with permission from authors and *Social Policy*, Winter 1984, Volume 14, Number 3, pp. 15–17.

"Regenerating Community" reprinted with permission from *Social Policy*, Winter 1987, Volume 17, Number 3, pp. 54–58.

"Killers Executed in Seperate Cases" reprinted with permission from the Associated Press as recorded in the *New York Times*, April 16, 1986, section B, page 9.

Index

Accountability, in human service systems, 101–3

Advocacy function, of medical organizations, 73–74

Advocacy vision, of society, 169

Aging population, 26–35; as commodity, 26–30, 31–35; criminal justice system and, 135–36; death and, 28, 34–35; gross national product (GNP) and, 28–29, 32–33; life crises and, 45; medicine and, 38, 56, 60, 64; "old" as problem, 26–30, 31–35; pension programs for, 32, 125; revising views of, 32–35; and welfare state, 32–33, 125

Agribusiness, 132

Alinsky, Saul, xii, 153–56

American Academy of Pediatrics, 10

American Federation of Teachers, 38

Antidemocratic systems, 47

Aries, Phillip, 30

Arrogance, and "professional problem," 19–20

Authority. *See* Power

Automobile accidents, as community problem, 83–84

Baldness, as problem, 29, 48

Banking institutions, 156

Barzun, Jacques, 17, 21

Bell, Daniel, 22

Bereavement counseling, 5–8, 11, 12, 14–15, 23, 96, 97, 125

Berger, Brigitte, 48

Berger, Peter, 17, 20

Birthing centers, 65

Blackhawk, 13–14

Blacks: as human sacrifice in criminal justice system, 139–44; poverty among, 140

Breastfeeding, bottlefeeding versus, 9–10, 11

Bronchial problems, as community problem, 84–85

Burnham, Walter Dean, 155

Capacity, as component of community, 170

Care: defined, x; as manifestation of community, x, 167; nature of, 38–39; as placebo, 59; value of, in economy, 34

Carter, Jimmy, 17
Celebration, as component of community, 171
Center for Urban Affairs and Policy Research at Northwestern University: community guide program, 119–22; study of healthful community, 71–79; study of need for health care services, 81–86; study of welfare dependency, 97–98
Centers for Disease Control (CDC), 138
Centuries of Childhood (Aries), 30
Child abuse, 48
Childbearing, as problem, 29, 65
Childhood: as concept, 30; as deficiency category, 30–31; institutionalization during, 8–9, 44
Choice, welfare state and, 128–29
Christian service, components of, xi–xii, 175–79
Civil rights movement, 16, 44
Clark, Kenneth, 142
Client councils, 20
Client populations: defined, 36; formation of, 10–11, 16; human service systems and, 91–100, 103–14; in medicine, 59–60; professionalism and, 10–11, 16–21, 36–37; service system need for, 91–100
Coding, 49–50, 75
Collective effort, as component of community, 170
Commodification: of aging population, 26–30, 31–35; of health care, 66, 67, 75
Community: associations in, 117–18, 154, 165–67, 169–70; belief in hospitable, 121–22; care as manifestation of, x, 167;

children in, 30–31; Christian service and, xi–xii, 175–79; community guide program, 119–22; components of, 170–72; and criminal justice system, 138–39, 147–48; declining sense of, 155–56; development of, 153–79; growth of authentic, xi; human service systems and, 104, 105–7, 112, 115–23, 161–68; including labeled population in, 119–23, 169; institutionalization practices and, 67, 115–23, 169; medicine and, xi, 66–79, 82–85, 87–88; nature of, 117–18; points of entry into, 119; policy of inclusion in, 122–23, 167–68; professionalism versus, 13–14, 30–35; recultivation of, 13–14; reinvestment practices of, 72–73, 159; separation of labeled population from, 115–17, 118; service economy as substitute for, x, 12, 30–35; and visions of society, 168–72; welfare state and, xi, 129–30
Community building, 153–79; Alinsky model for, 153–56; neighborhoods in, 81–86, 153–54, 157–58, 160; obstacles to, 154–56; private sector in, 155–56, 159–60; public sector in, 158–59
Community Reinvestment Act, 159
Community Services Society of New York, 164
Confessions of a Medical Heretic (Mendelsohn), xii
Consumer movement, 50;

medicine and, 56, 58, 66–67, 75–77
Convalescent homes, 108
Convening function, of medical organizations, 74
Corporations, "professional problem" and, 18
Counterproductivity: of criminal justice system, 146; of human service systems, 109; of professionalism, 7–12, 41–43
Criminal justice system, xi, 19, 135–49; aging population and, 135–36; allopathic approach to, 137–38; blacks in, 139–44; care and, 39; community and, 138–39, 147–48; criticism of, 41, 146; death and, 136, 143–44; health model for, 138–39; human sacrifice and, 139–44; iatrogenesis and, 138, 164; incarceration policy and, 145–49; law school graduates and, 39, 96; poverty and, 140, 146–49; rehabilitation process in, 135–39. *See also* Institutionalization
Cults, 21

Death: aging population and, 28, 34–35; bereavement counseling and, 5–8, 11, 12, 14–15, 23, 97, 125; causes of, 35; in criminal justice system, 136, 143–44; impact of doctor strikes on, 9; medicine and, 9, 60; and mortality, 64, 69; need creation based on, 5–8, 12, 14–15, 23, 96–97; phases of, 45
Deere, John, invention of plow, 3–4, 5, 7, 9, 14

Deficiency approach: to aging, 26–30, 31–35; to childhood, 30–31; to human service systems, 103–4, 111–12, 122–23; to medicine, 59, 75, 76–77; to need, 26–35, 43, 46–52, 103–4
Dependency: human services and, 122–23; interdependence versus, 123; welfare, 72–73, 97–98, 105, 112, 125–26. *See also* Client populations
Developmental disabilities. *See* Labeling, impact of
Dewar, Thomas, 50
Doctors. *See* Physicians
Dog bites, as community problem, 82
"Do no harm" provision, xi, 101–14. *See also* Iatrogenesis
Drug use, 7, 21, 68
Dubos, Rene, 57, 70, 71, 72, 75

Economic power, of medical organizations, 74
Educare, 38
Education: health care, 66, 75; of lawyers, 39, 96; service economy and, 94–95, 98–99. *See also* Schools
Efficiency, and "professional problem," 18–19
Elderly. *See* Aging population
Ethics: accountability and, 101–3; Hippocratic oath, 101–2; medicine and, xi, 56, 58, 101–2, 111

Federal Health Care Financing Administration, 57
Fitness, 65
Food and Drug Administration, 110, 111

Franchising industry, 94–95
Fuchs, Victor, 57, 70, 72, 75

Gandhi, 175, 176
General Motors, 18
Ginzberg, Eli, 17
Glazer, Nathan, 17
Goodman, Paul, 127
Government: in community
    building, 158–59;
    "professional problem"
    and, 17–18; role in service
    economy, 37, 93
Greenhouses, community, 84–86
Grief. *See* Bereavement
    counseling
Gross national product (GNP):
    aging population and,
    28–29, 32–33; goods versus
    service production in,
    28–29, 91–92; importance
    of, 91–92, 162; and
    medicine, 59; pressure to
    increase size of, 22; service
    economy as part of, 7,
    18–19, 22, 36–37, 43, 92,
    97–98, 162, 164, 177; value
    of caring in, 34
Group homes, 108, 115, 121–22
Guilt, 21

Haiman, Franklyn, xiii
Halfway houses, 108
Health alternatives, 12, 64–66,
    68, 71
Health care system. *See* Medicine
Health education, 66, 75
Health model: community,
    81–86; criminal justice
    system, 138–39
Hippocratic oath, 101–2
Home birth movement, 65
Hospice movement, 12, 65
Human service systems, x,
    91–132; accountability in,
    101–3; clients in, 103–14;

community and, 104,
    105–7, 112, 115–23,
    161–68; deficiency
    approach to, 103–4,
    111–12, 122–23; iatrogenic
    practices of, 102–14;
    incarceration policy and,
    146–49; labeling and,
    103–14; model for
    evaluating, 109–12; need
    for client populations,
    91–100, 103–14; policy
    options for, 111–12;
    poverty and, xi, 97–98,
    108–9, 111–12, 146–49;
    problems in design of,
    161–64; public budgets
    and, 105; in service
    economy, 92–100;
    simultaneous use of many
    programs in, 107–9, 110;
    trade-offs and, 105; welfare
    state and, xi, 97–98, 108–9,
    111–12

Iatrogenesis: criminal justice
    system and, 138, 164; in
    human service systems,
    102–14; in medicine, 41,
    101–2, 109, 138; and
    "professional problem,"
    20–21, 24, 41
Illich, Ivan, xii, 8, 17, 20, 41, 57
Individualization, 44–46
Informality, as component of
    community, 170–71
Institutionalization: of aging
    population, 33–34; of
    children, 8–9, 44;
    community and, 67,
    115–23, 169; negative
    impact of, 108. *See also*
    Criminal justice system

James, William, 142
Jefferson, Thomas, 175, 176

Jeremiah, 175
Jesus Christ, 176–79
Judicare, 39
Juvenile correction institutions, 8–9

King, Martin Luther, Jr., 99, 142
Kübler-Ross, Elizabeth, 45

Labeling, impact of: community and, 115–23, 169; and criminal justice system, 139; in human service systems, 103–14
Lactation technology, 9–10, 11
La Leche League, 9–10, 11
Lasch, Christopher, 20–21
Last One Over the Wall (Miller), xiii
Law schools, 39, 96
Learning disabilities, 48
Life expectancy, 28
Lilly, Eli, 7, 68
Love, 39, 40

Management, health care, 65–66
Marx, Karl, 160
McKeown, Thomas, 70, 72, 75, 138
Medicaid, 9, 18, 56
Medical insurance, 67
Medical Nemesis (Illich), 20
Medicare, 38, 56
Medicine, 55–88; aging population and, 38, 56, 60, 64; allopathic approach to, 64, 65, 68, 75, 138; antidiagnosis approach to, 75–77; care and, 38; client populations in, 59–60; as commodity, 66, 67, 75; community involvement and, xi, 66–79, 82–85, 87–88; consumer participation in, 56, 58, 66–67, 75–77; cost control,

57, 58; cost control in, 56; criticism of, 40, 138; deficiency approach to, 59, 75, 76–77; defining health problems in, 82–85; drug use and, 7, 21, 68; elements of medical system, 65–66; environment and, 70–79, 81–89; equal access to care, 56, 57; ethics and, xi, 56, 58, 101–2, 111; health alternatives and, 12, 64–66, 68, 71; "health care crisis" and, 55–59; Hippocratic oath, 101–2; hospice movement and, 12, 65; iatrogenesis and, 41, 101–2, 109, 138; impact on health, 9, 57, 63–64; and lactation technology, 9–10, 11; multility vs. unitility in, 85–86; politics and, 58–62, 80–88; poverty and, 9, 18, 56, 64, 67, 71, 72, 80, 124–25; preventive health care movement, 56–57, 58; "professional problem" and, 18, 56; quality of care, 56, 57; reasons for hospitalization, 81–82; reforming, 56–58; technology and, 8, 60; in welfare state, 124–25. *See also* Physicians
Mendelsohn, Robert, xii
Menopause, as problem, 29
Mental health system, criticism of, 41
Miller, Jerome, xiii, 8–9, 139
Mirage of Health, The (Dubos), 70
Mourning. *See* Bereavement counseling
Multility, unitility versus, 85–86

National Center for Institutions and Alternatives, xiii

192 · *Index*

National Center for Neighborhood Enterprise, xiii
National Center on Institutions
and Alternatives, 139
Need: deficiency approach to,
26–35, 43, 46–52, 103–4;
disabling characteristics of,
46–52; manufacturing of,
42–52; and medicine, 59;
nature of, 39–40;
professionalized
assumptions regarding,
43–46; as raw material of
service economy, 23–24,
29–32, 39–52, 95–98; of
service providers, 29–32,
42–52, 97–98
Neighborhoods, in community
building process, 81–86,
153–54, 157–58, 160
Neuhaus, Richard, 17, 20
Northwestern University. *See*
Center for Urban Affairs
and Policy Research at
Northwestern University

Obstetricians, 9–10
"Old," as problem, 26–30, 31–35.
See also Aging population

Parent groups, 20
Patient advocacy services, 19–20,
125
Pediatricians, 9–10
Pension programs, 32, 125
People's Medical Society, 66–67
Personnel, of medical
organizations, 74
Physicians: classification of
patients by, 59; and
lactation technology, 9–10;
strikes, impact of, 9. *See
also* Medicine
Plow: impact of, 3–4, 5, 7, 9, 14;
professionalism compared
with, 5–8

Policy: community and, 122–23,
168; for human service
systems, 111–12;
incarceration, 145–49; for
welfare state, 131–32
Politics: and medicine, 58–62,
80–88; and service
economy, 37–52
Poverty: of aging population,
32–33, 125; allocation of
welfare funds and, 72–73,
97–98, 105, 112, 125–26,
164; among blacks, 140;
criminal justice system and,
140, 146–49; human service
systems and, xi, 97–98,
108–9, 111–12, 146–49; and
importance of community
building, 153–60; and
institutionalization of
children, 44; medical care
and, 9, 18, 56, 64, 67, 71,
72, 80, 124–25;
"professional problem" and,
18; service economy and,
93–95. *See also* Welfare state
Power: medicine and, 61–62,
75–77; professionalism
and, 48–50; welfare state
and, 99
Preventive health care, 56–57, 58
Private sector, in community
building, 155–56, 159–60
Professionalism, x–xi, 3–52; and
aging population, 26–30,
31–32; arrogance and,
19–20; in bereavement
counseling, 5–8, 11, 12,
14–15, 23, 96, 97, 125; care
and, x, 38–39; and
childhood, 30–31; in
Christian service, 178–79;
and client population,
10–11, 16–21, 36–37;
community versus, 13–14,
30–35; counterproductivity

of, 7–12, 41–43; criticisms
of, 40–52; disabling
characteristics of, 46–52;
distance from client and,
47; goods versus service
technology and, 7–8, 12,
28–29; government and,
17–18; and growth of
service economy, 22,
28–32; iatrogenic argument
against, 20–21, 24, 41;
inefficiency and, 18–19; in
medicine, 18, 56; needs of
caregivers, 29–32, 42–52,
97–98; power and, 48–50;
"professional problem"
and, 16–25, 41; pyramiding
of services in, 7; and
"reform" of professional
practice, 21–25; remedial
tools and, 47–48; resistance
to, 9–10, 11, 16–25, 44, 50;
and unmet needs, 23–24,
29–32, 39–52, 95–98
Programmatic social services, 125
"Protectionist" legislation, 132
Public sector, in community
building, 158–59

Recluse management, 23, 96–97
Reform: medical, 56–58; of
professional practice,
21–25
"Removal trauma," 48
Reveille for Radicals (Alinsky), xii
Rodale, Robert, xii–xiii
Rodale Press, xii–xiii
*Role of Medicine: Dream, Mirage or
Nemesis* (McKeown), 70
Roosevelt, Franklin D., 98

Sacrifice, society's need for,
139–44
Sauk County, Wisconsin, 4–5,
13–14
Sauk Indians, 4–5, 13–14

Schools: bereavement counseling
in, 14–15; and concept of
childhood, 31; criticism of,
40; law, 39, 96; medicine
and, 66; servicing ideology
and, 50–51; teachers, need
for, 38. *See also* Education
Schumacher, E. F., 3, 7, 8, 13
Self-care, 65
Self-help movement, 16, 19–20
Service economy, x, 92–100;
apolitical ideology of,
37–52; characteristics of,
36–37, 93–98;
counterproductivity of,
7–12, 41–43; criticisms of,
40–52; education and,
94–95, 98–99; extent of,
22, 26; government role in,
37, 93; and gross national
product (GNP), 7, 18–19,
22, 36–37, 43, 92, 97–98,
162, 163–64, 177; growth
of, 22, 28–32, 92; "hidden
curriculum" of, 10–12;
ideological roots of, xi–xii;
industrialization of, 94–95;
and loss of knowledge,
9–10; move toward, 92;
poverty and, 93–95;
pyramiding of services in,
7; role of care in, 38–39; as
substitute for community,
x, 12, 30–35; in Sweden,
163–64; unmet needs and,
23–24, 29–32, 39–52,
95–98
Smith, Adam, 160
Snow, Judith, 143
Social Security system, 32
Social welfare. *See* Welfare state
Society, community in visions of,
168–72
Space, in medical organizations,
74
Specialization, 45–46

"Specific counterproductivity" (Illich), 8, 41
Stories, as component of community, 171
Summons to Life, A (Woodson), 139
Sweden, 163–64

Tax revolts, 93
Therapeutic vision, of society, 168–69
Thomas, Daniel Morris, 143–44
Thomas, Lewis, 28, 63
Thompson, Marion, 10
Tocqueville, Alexis de, 117
Tragedy, as component of community, 171–72
Twain, Mark, 64, 103

Unitility, multility versus, 85–86
Universities, as service institutions, 177–78

War, 142
Welfare state, xi, 124–32; aging population and, 32–33, 125; allocation of funds, 72–73, 97–98, 105, 112, 125–26, 164; community and, xi, 129–30; deregulation proposal, 131–32; elements of, 124–27; human service systems and, xi, 97–98, 108–9, 111–12; and needs of caregivers, 97–98; as outgrowth of other systems, 126–27; public policy and, 131–32; spheres for free action versus, 127–31. *See also* Poverty
Wholistic health, 65
Who Shall Live (Fuchs), 70
Women's liberation movement, 44
Woodson, Robert, xiii, 139
Work: changing nature of, 92–95; importance of, 91–92, 98–100